KAY LAUREL

Becoming Mama

A Memoir of Strength, Softness, and the Making of a
Mother

First published by Cedar Ink Press 2026

First edition

ISBN: 9798994548301

This book was professionally typeset on Reedsy.
Find out more at reedsy.com

For my daughter.
For the one who made me a mother.
Your life changed mine.

Contents

Acknowledgments

This book exists because of the people who stood with me as I was *Becoming Mama*.

First, to my daughter. You will not read this for a long time, but everything here traces back to you. You changed me in ways I am still discovering. You softened me and strengthened me at the same time. You gave shape to hopes I once held carefully and taught me how to carry them with courage. Thank you for choosing me, for trusting me, and for being exactly who you are.

To your dad. Thank you for standing beside me in the moments that mattered most. For listening when things were hard, for holding steady when I felt unsure, and for choosing our family again and again. This story is shaped by partnership, by shared resolve, and by the quiet ways you showed up long before you were asked. I am grateful to build this life with you.

To my parents. Thank you for the foundation you gave me, for the ways you modeled care, protection, and resilience long before I had language for them. Thank you for the sacrifices that went unseen, the patience that held, and the love that remained steady. Becoming a mother has deepened my gratitude for you in ways I never could have understood before.

To the nurses, doctors, and professionals who offered skill, kindness, and humanity at pivotal moments. Some of you will never know how much your presence mattered. In rooms filled with uncertainty, your steadiness, compassion, and care made all the difference. Thank you for showing up with both expertise and heart.

To the friends who checked in without expectations, who listened without trying to fix, who held space when words were heavy and celebrated the small victories with me. Your presence mattered more than you know. Thank you for meeting me where I was and reminding me I did not have to carry everything alone.

To the women who shared their motherhood stories with honesty and courage. Your willingness to speak the truth about motherhood, without polish or performance, made this book possible. You reminded me that no one walks this path alone, even when it sometimes feels that way.

To the professionals, mentors, and colleagues who shaped my understanding of care, boundaries, and resilience. Your work and insight live quietly in these pages, informing the way I see families, systems, and the courage it takes to show up with intention.

And to the reader. Thank you for being here. Thank you for trusting these words, for seeing yourself somewhere within them, and for allowing this story to sit alongside your own. However you arrived at motherhood, whatever shape your journey has taken, your presence here matters.

This book was written in moments borrowed from real life. It is imperfect, unfinished, and deeply sincere.

Like motherhood itself.

Thank you to everyone who made space for it to exist.

Introduction

If motherhood came with an instruction manual, I imagine it would be worn thin in the places that matter most. The pages would be soft from use, corners folded down at moments of panic or exhaustion. Margins would be crowded with notes written quickly, questions circled, and answers crossed out. Some sections would be smudged from tears or early-morning coffee spills. And just when you reached for the page you needed most, the words would blur, the ink faded, and the guidance incomplete. Not because you failed to read it correctly, but because motherhood itself refuses to be fully explained.

Motherhood does not arrive neatly packaged or perfectly timed. It does not wait for certainty. It does not follow a script. It does not begin with a pregnancy test or a due date or even the first cry that changes everything. It begins long before that. It begins in the quiet wondering. In the imagining you barely let yourself linger in. In the small internal shift that happens when you realize your life may one day revolve around someone else's.

My path to motherhood did not follow the order I once assumed it would. It was not clean or predictable or easy to explain. I was a social worker who had spent years holding other people's stories. I sat with families in their most fragile moments. I witnessed resilience and devastation, love and loss, repair and rupture. I learned what helps people survive and what breaks them open. I thought that knowledge might prepare me. I believed that experience would steady me.

And still, when it came time to build a family of my own, I felt unprepared in ways no degree or training could touch.

I had a body that did not always cooperate. PCOS complicated the assumptions I had carried quietly for years. My love story unfolded out of order, shaped by timing, fear, hope, and honesty. I became a mother before I ever became a wife. I entered pregnancy with reverence and anxiety braided together. I entered labor carrying strength I did not yet recognize as my own. And when my daughter finally arrived, after fear and pain and hope collided in ways I could not have imagined, I felt myself split open and reassembled in the same breath.

Motherhood did not gently transform me. It stretched me. It demanded parts of me I had never needed before. It softened me and hardened me in different places at the same time. It asked me to function through exhaustion while feeling more alive than I ever had. It required patience and protection, surrender and vigilance, grief and gratitude, all at once.

This is the contradiction no one fully prepares you for. Motherhood can feel overwhelming and gentle in the same moment. It is bone-deep tiredness followed by a single look that rearranges your understanding of love. It is missing the version of yourself you once were while falling deeply into the life you are living now. It is learning that you can be undone and still be exactly where you are meant to be.

Along the way, I learned something that changed everything. There is no correct order. There is no universal blueprint. There is no single way to become a mother. There are countless paths. Some are smooth. Some are painful. Some are shaped by loss before they are shaped by joy. Some are chosen deliberately. Some arrive unexpectedly. All of them are real. All of them are worthy. All of them deserve compassion.

This book is not an instruction manual.

It is not a checklist.

It is not here to tell you how to do this right.

It is more like a hand at your back when you feel unsteady.

A quiet voice reminding you that you are not alone.

A place to sit for a moment when becoming feels heavy.

This book is for the mama in the middle of it.

The one who is tired.

The one who is trying.

The one who is doing her best even when it does not feel like enough.

The one learning that motherhood is not about perfection, but about presence.

You are here, in the beautiful and impossible work of becoming.

There was no wrong turn that brought you to this moment.

No version of your story that disqualifies you.

Welcome. You made it.

And however you arrived here, I hope you know this already.

It was enough.

1

The Knowing

Before I ever became a mother, I learned how to hold other people's stories.

I learned how to sit with grief that did not belong to me, how to cradle hope that felt too fragile to name, how to witness parenting journeys that were unfolding in real time, messy and imperfect and deeply human. I learned how to listen to what was said and, more importantly, to what was not. I learned to notice the way a child's shoulders tighten when a parent enters the room, the way a mother's voice shifts when she is trying not to cry, the way silence can signal safety for one person and danger for another.

As a social worker, I was trained to slow down. To resist the urge to rush toward answers simply because they felt comforting. To sit with discomfort long enough for truth to surface. I learned that real care does not always come with solutions. Sometimes it comes with presence.

I did not enter this work thinking it was preparation for motherhood. At least not consciously. I stepped into it because I wanted to help. Because I believed in protection and repair. I believed that children deserved to be seen fully, not reduced to case numbers or court summaries, and that parents deserved to be met with honesty rather than judgment. I believed that experiences carry weight, and that when they are met with compassion, that weight becomes more bearable. My role meant staying when things were uncomfortable, listening without flinching, holding space without rushing, and honoring truth even when it was complicated. I did not always have the power to change outcomes, but I could make sure families felt seen while living through some of the hardest moments of their lives. I believed, deeply, that mattered.

What I did not understand then was how deeply those lessons would settle. I assumed they would live neatly within my workday, contained by office walls and courtrooms and case notes I closed at the end of the day. I believed I could witness suffering, learn its patterns, and leave it behind when I went home. I did not yet know that the lessons I was absorbing were not just professional tools, but quiet imprints, reshaping the way I listened, the way I showed up, the way I learned to tolerate uncertainty without turning away.

Slowly, almost unnoticeably, what I learned at work began to move into the private corners of my life. It influenced how I noticed people, how I measured safety, how I understood the difference between control and care. I was learning, long before motherhood arrived, that love is not proven through certainty or perfection, but through attunement, presence, and the willingness to remain when things feel hard. What I was learning in offices and courtrooms, in quiet rooms thick with truth and vulnerability, echoed something deeply familiar.

What I would come to realize later is that this kind of preparation does not belong exclusively to any profession. It does not only happen in offices, hospitals, or courtrooms. It happens in ordinary lives, often without announcement. It happens when you learn how to care deeply for someone else. When you learn how to stay present during hard conversations. When you learn how to sit with discomfort instead of rushing to fix it. Some women learn this through caregiving roles, through siblings, through illness, through loss, through loving partners or friends through seasons that stretch them thin. Some learn it through their own childhoods, by watching what was done well and what they promised themselves they would do differently. No matter the path, many of us arrive at motherhood already carrying a lifetime of emotional muscle memory we did not realize we were building.

You do not need a particular background, training, or title to recognize this feeling. Most mothers can trace their becoming back to moments long before children, moments that quietly shaped the way they would one day love. Moments that taught them patience, restraint, and how deeply they could care without having control. Motherhood rarely begins at conception. It begins earlier, in the ways you learn to love, to protect, to stay. By the time a child arrives, most of us have already been practicing, whether we knew it or not.

It took time to recognize why that familiarity felt so rooted. Why the lessons unfolding in my career did not feel entirely new, but remembered. The patience I was practicing, the restraint I was learning, the way I was being taught to sit with emotion without trying to manage it away, all of it traced back to something familiar. Something foundational. Before I ever learned these skills in a professional setting, I had lived them. I had been shaped by them.

I learned them first in my childhood. .

My mother was steady in a way that felt rare and grounding. She listened without interruption, without fixing, without judgment. I remember sitting in the passenger seat while she drove, unloading the worries and hurts of my younger years. She never rushed me. She never dismissed the intensity of feelings that come with being small in a world that often feels too loud. From her, I learned that love does not need to announce itself to be powerful. Sometimes it arrives quietly, through presence alone.

My father showed me another expression of care. His compassion was shaped by his work as a police officer, carried home in quiet, intentional ways. He believed deeply in protection, not as authority, but as responsibility. He never allowed his work to harden him. I remember him coming home in uniform, exhausted in ways I did not yet understand, and still kneeling down to ask about my day. Through him, I learned that strength could be firm without being cruel, that boundaries could exist alongside tenderness. Watching him serve the community taught me that love sometimes looks like stepping in, speaking up, and refusing to look away when something is wrong.

Together, my parents modeled balance. They showed me softness paired with courage, intuition paired with decisiveness. One taught me how to hold space. The other taught me how to stand firmly within it. Long before I imagined becoming a mother myself, I was absorbing a blueprint for the kind of parent I hoped to be someday. Not perfect. But present. Not all-knowing. But willing.

Still, nothing prepared me for the way social work would deepen that understanding.

Working nearly a decade in child abuse and neglect exposed me to the farthest edges of family life. It pulled back the curtain on the parts of parenting that rarely make it into conversation, the places where love and fear coexist, where good intentions collide with exhaustion, and where survival sometimes takes precedence over softness. I learned quickly that love does not always arrive in gentle forms. Sometimes it comes tangled in court dates and safety plans, in whispered disclosures shared only after trust has been earned, in silences so heavy they seem to press against the walls. I learned that families are rarely simple, and that care is often complicated by history, trauma, and circumstances no one chooses.

I sat across from parents who loved their children fiercely and were still struggling to keep them safe. Parents who wanted better but were carrying more than their nervous systems could hold. I watched how trauma rewires the body, how it sharpens reactions and dulls patience, how it turns small stressors into overwhelming threats. I saw how exhaustion erodes even the strongest intentions, how cycles repeat when there is no space for rest, regulation, or repair. And I learned that none of this makes someone unloving. It makes them human.

I did not have children then, but motherhood was already shaping me.

I watched parents succeed and fail in ways that felt deeply human, never cleanly divided into right and wrong. I watched systems designed to protect sometimes help and harm in the same breath. I learned that love alone is not always enough without support, accountability, and the willingness to change. These years taught me that motherhood is not instinct alone. It is intention. It is humility. It is the ongoing work of learning yourself as much as you are learning your child.

Being a social worker without children felt like learning a language fluently without ever speaking it in your own home.

I could read infant cues without hesitation, teach attachment theory with confidence, coach parents through crisis, and map developmental milestones by memory. I knew the words, the frameworks, and the research. But at the end of the day, I went home to a quiet house. No bedtime routines waiting to be honored. No sticky fingerprints on the windows. No small shoes by the door or tiny voices calling my name.

I loved my work deeply, but there was an ache that lived alongside it. I carried other people's children in my heart, worried about them long after my workday ended, replayed conversations, wondered if the support that was put in place would be enough. And in the quiet of my own home, I wondered what kind of mother I would be if the chance ever came.

That question followed me quietly. It folded itself into my life the way the hardest cases did. Always present. Rarely spoken aloud.

Even then, there was certainty. Not urgency. Not desperation. Just a steady awareness. For me, motherhood was not a question of if, but when.

I knew the risks. I knew how fragile stability could be. I knew that love without attunement could still leave wounds. I knew that even the most well-intentioned parents could break under pressure. And because I knew all of that, I did not approach motherhood with romantic illusions.

What I carried instead was reverence.

Before I ever tried to conceive, I understood how high the stakes were. I understood that parenting would demand accountability, not perfection. That it would require me to confront parts of myself I had not yet fully met. My career did not scare me away from motherhood. It humbled me toward

9

it.

It taught me that awareness matters more than confidence. That repair matters more than getting it right the first time. That showing up matters more than having all the answers. I did not assume instincts would save me. I hoped intention would steady me.

And still, there was longing.

I watched friends move through milestones. Engagements. Pregnancies. Baby showers. I celebrated them honestly, while quietly acknowledging the space between where I was and where I hoped to be. I had a career I believed in. A relationship grounded in love. A home that felt safe. And yet, there was no child of my own.

No one tells you how strange it feels to want something deeply while understanding exactly how complicated it can be.

But beneath it all, there was trust. Trust that the years I spent working with other families were shaping me. Trust that I was gathering empathy and restraint, courage and humility, for a role that would ask everything of me.

When I finally reached the point of wanting a child of my own, I did not walk into motherhood blindly. I walked in aware. Aware of how much it would change me. Aware of how much grace it would require. Aware that love would demand both strength and surrender.

My career did not make me a perfect mother.

It made me a conscious one.

Long before my daughter arrived, I was already learning how to show up for her. Motherhood did not begin with a pregnancy test for me. It began in awareness. In observation. In years of learning what children need and what parents carry. It began in humility and longing and the quiet decision to become someone capable of holding another person's whole world.

And when the time came, I rose to meet it with everything I had learned, everything I was still learning, and a hope that had been growing quietly all along.

For the Mama in It Right Now:

If you are surrounded by other people's stories, holding their pain, their fears, and their parenting struggles while quietly wondering what kind of mother you will be someday, pause and breathe. It is not a flaw to feel both drawn to motherhood and uncertain about it. There is no invisible clock you are racing against, no checklist you must complete before you are allowed to imagine yourself in that role.

You do not need to have all the answers yet. Motherhood is not something you prepare for by achieving perfection or certainty. It is something you grow into, slowly, through care, awareness, and empathy. The compassion you offer now, the way you listen without fixing, the way you sit with discomfort and show up anyway, is already shaping the kind of parent you will become.

If you find yourself comparing your path to others, wondering if you are "behind" or taking too long to arrive where everyone else seems to be, remember that readiness is not measured by timing. It is measured by the capacity to hold complexity, to love without guarantees, and to remain present even when the outcome is unknown.

You do not need to have lived motherhood to honor it with tenderness. You are already practicing the skills it requires. The patience you extend, the boundaries you learn to set, the care you give to others and to yourself are not separate from motherhood. They are part of it.

Trust that the version of you who is listening, learning, and becoming right now is enough. You are not waiting to begin. You already have.

What I Wish I Knew Then:

- Motherhood is not a race, and you are not behind.
- The patience, empathy, and resilience you already carry are seeds of motherhood.
- You don't need to "prove" readiness. You just need to arrive.
- You will not have all the answers. You were never supposed to.

2

The Body That Complicated Hope

When you are young, you trust your body without question.

You assume it will do what bodies are supposed to do. That when the time comes, it will cooperate. You don't analyze your cycles or wonder what they mean. You don't think about ovulation or hormones or timing. Fertility is something you take for granted, a future certainty you assume will be waiting when you are ready to reach for it.

For many women, that unquestioned trust does not disappear all at once. It erodes quietly, often after the first moment your body surprises you. A missed period. A complication. A diagnosis you didn't expect. A pregnancy that doesn't unfold the way you imagined it would. Or simply the realization that the body you have lived inside of for years has its own agenda. Whether it arrives through infertility, loss, medical intervention, or pregnancy itself, there is often a moment when certainty cracks. When you realize your body is not something you command, but something you instead must learn how to listen to.

Almost every mother I know can point to that reckoning.

13

The moment when control gave way to vulnerability. When assumptions softened into awareness. For some, it comes before conception. For others, during pregnancy. For many, it arrives in labor, postpartum, or in the quiet realization that motherhood is asking more of your body than you ever anticipated. The details are different, but the experience is shared. Motherhood, in one form or another, teaches us that trust is not blind. It is earned, rebuilt, and renegotiated as our bodies change and our lives expand. However it comes, it marks the end of assumption and the beginning of listening.

I didn't think much about my reproductive body back then. It existed quietly in the background of my life, managed and regulated in a way that felt responsible, even freeing.

Birth control had been part of my life for nearly a decade. It kept things predictable. Controlled. Neat. It promised freedom from surprise and allowed me to move through adulthood without thinking too much about my reproductive body. At least, that was the story I told myself. What I didn't recognize until much later was how disconnected I had become from my own rhythms and my own emotional landscape.

Over time, I started to feel unfamiliar to myself. My reactions felt sharper than they should have been. My emotions swung in ways that didn't match my circumstances. I felt like I was watching myself from a distance, trying to make sense of how easily overwhelmed I had become. I chalked it up to stress. To work. It took me longer than it should have to consider that the birth control I had trusted so implicitly might be shaping me in ways I didn't recognize.

When I finally raised those concerns with my doctor, the answer came quickly and quietly, delivered with the kind of clinical calm that makes you question whether you are supposed to feel unsettled by it. Because of my history of migraines, estrogen-based birth control was not recommended for me. It never had been. She said it plainly, without drama, without apology, as if this information had always existed somewhere in my chart, waiting for me to notice it myself.

She declined to refill my prescription and began listing non-hormonal alternatives, her voice steady and efficient, already moving on to next steps. The conversation shifted forward with ease, but I stayed stuck in the space she had just cracked open. Ten years. A decade on estrogen-based birth control that carried a significant risk for someone with my history of migraines. A decade of emotional volatility that I had blamed on stress or personality or circumstance. A decade of side effects I had normalized. All of it was suddenly reframed in a single sentence.

What unsettled me most was not the change itself, but how ordinary it was treated. There was no acknowledgment of the time that had passed, no pause to reflect on what that information might mean for my body, my emotions, or my sense of trust in my own experience or my medical provider. It was handled like a minor adjustment, a simple course correction. And maybe medically, it was. But emotionally, it felt like realizing you have been walking with a rock in your shoe for years and only now being told you never had to.

I left that appointment with new information and an unex-pected grief. Grief for the version of myself who had spent years feeling disconnected from her own emotions, wondering why she felt so reactive, so unsteady, so unlike herself. Grief for the trust I had placed so fully in something I had never been taught to question. And beneath that grief, a quiet resolve began to form. If I was going to move forward, toward motherhood or anything else, I needed to start listening to my body more closely. I needed to stop assuming discomfort was normal just because it was familiar.

That appointment marked the beginning of a shift. Not just in medication, but in awareness. It was the first time I understood how easily women are taught to accept explanations that do not fully explain, to adjust instead of question, to live with side effects instead of asking whether they are necessary. And it was the moment I realized that becoming a mother might first require becoming an advocate for myself.

Going off hormonal birth control felt like relief at first. A quiet exhale I hadn't realized I'd been holding for years. Almost immediately, I recognized myself again. My emotions settled into something steadier, something I could trust. I could feel deeply without feeling overtaken by my own reactions. Sadness came and went without swallowing me whole. Joy felt clean instead of jittery. I felt clearer. More grounded. More me.

It was as if I had been living slightly outside my body for years and had finally returned.

For the first time in a long time, my thoughts felt like they belonged to me. My moods made sense. My inner world felt quieter, more predictable. I moved through my days with a sense of alignment that was subtle but unmistakable. I told myself this was what balance was supposed to feel like. This was what listening to your body looked like.

And then my cycle disappeared.

Without the structure of synthetic hormones, my body revealed its own unpredictability. Periods came late or not at all. Weeks stretched into months. Tracking my cycle became guesswork. Apps offered cheerful predictions that meant nothing when day thirty came and went without explanation.

Each skipped cycle carried a familiar mix of confusion and unease, the kind that settles low in your chest and lingers.

What had first felt like freedom slowly began to feel like uncertainty.

I watched my body closely, trying to read its signals, trying to understand its rhythm. I told myself to be patient. To trust the process. To remember that bodies need time to recalibrate. But patience is harder when you are waiting without a map. When there is no pattern to anchor yourself to. When every symptom feels ambiguous and every absence feels loud.

The pregnancy scares started quietly.

A late period. A flicker of panic. A test taken more out of fear than hope. The first one landed on Father's Day, of all days. We bought a test, our movements casual, careful, as if naming the possibility might summon it. On the way out of the store, we ran into a former colleague of mine who announced her second pregnancy with easy joy, the kind that fills a conversation without effort. I smiled. I congratulated her. I held space for her excitement while something tightened inside me.

I remember thinking how strange it is to carry two completely different emotional worlds at once. To celebrate someone else's certainty while bracing yourself for your own unknown.

The test was negative. Relief came first, sharp and immediate. Then confusion followed, quieter but heavier. My body, it seemed, was adjusting. Or misfiring. Or doing something entirely its own, outside my ability to predict or control. I told myself this was normal. That it didn't mean anything yet. That one late cycle wasn't a pattern.

But it wasn't just one.

More scares followed. Another long cycle that stretched

uncomfortably into a friend's wedding weekend out of state. I smiled through photos and speeches while silently stepping away from the noise to call my doctor. I explained that it had been weeks longer than usual and my period hadn't yet arrived. That I wasn't sure what was happening. That I just needed reassurance. We scheduled an appointment for the following week. I needed answers. The uncertainty had grown louder than my patience.

When I finally sat across from my doctor and explained what had been happening, she listened carefully and then began outlining next steps in a tone that was calm and measured, meant to steady rather than alarm. This doctor was not the one who had originally prescribed my birth control. That mattered to me. After learning that estrogen-based contraception had never been recommended for someone with my history of migraines, I needed a second opinion. I wanted fresh eyes and a new provider.

She ordered lab work to check my hormone levels, explaining that it would give us a clear picture of how my body was functioning without synthetic hormones regulating it. Alongside the blood work, she recommended a transvaginal ultrasound, a closer look at my ovaries and uterus to rule out cysts or other structural issues that could be interfering with my cycle.

There is nothing quite like a transvaginal ultrasound to humble you. The technician wheeled in a wand that looked like it belonged in a science fiction movie and asked, with startling cheer, whether I wanted to insert it myself or have her do it.

There is no correct answer to that question. None.

Do I want to awkwardly stab myself with medical equipment while a stranger watches? Absolutely not. Do I want a stranger to do it for me while I stare at the ceiling tiles and contemplate every choice that has led me to this moment? Also no.

These tests, the doctor explained, were standard. A way to gather information, not jump to conclusions. Hormone imbalances can disrupt ovulation. Ovarian cysts can interfere with regular cycles. The body, especially after years of hormonal birth control, sometimes needs help finding its footing again.

Then she paused, as if sensing the fear growing quietly in my chest.

She reassured me that I was not presenting with the classic symptoms she would expect if something more serious were happening. I was not overweight. I was not experiencing some of the outward signs often associated with more severe hormonal disorders. Based on my history and how I presented, she told me she genuinely believed the results would come back normal. That this was likely my body recalibrating. That the tests were precautionary, not predictive.

I nodded. I thanked her. I told myself to breathe.

But there is something unsettling about your body becoming a question mark, even when reassurance is offered freely. There is a quiet vulnerability in lying back for imaging, in waiting for numbers to come back on a chart, in realizing that no matter how much you understand the process, some part of you is still hoping your body will simply prove it knows what it is doing.

The tests were ordered to offer clarity.

But what they also offered was a moment of reckoning.

That cycle stretched to sixty-three days.

Sixty-three days of waiting. Watching. Wondering. Sixty-three days of scanning my body for signs that never quite arrived.

The diagnosis came soon after. Polycystic Ovary Syndrome (PCOS).

It did not come from the doctor who had first ordered my labs. She unfortunately had left her position and moved away before we could follow up, and I found myself explaining my history all over again to a new provider. By the time the diagnosis was confirmed, it was a third medical professional sitting across from me. He reviewed the results that had already begun to reshape how I understood my body.

The words landed heavier than I expected, settling some-where between my chest and my stomach. PCOS explained the irregular cycles, the long stretches of waiting, the sense that my body was moving to a rhythm no calendar could predict. It gave language to the unpredictability I had been living inside for months. In that way, it was clarifying. But clarity does not always bring comfort.

This provider spoke even more clinically than the first. He explained that my hormone levels and ultrasound findings aligned with PCOS, that this was likely something I had been living with for years without knowing it. He recommended a non-hormonal birth control option to help regulate my periods and added, almost casually, that when I was ready to get pregnant, I could come back for a Clomid prescription. As if that future were a simple switch to flip. As if readiness alone would determine timing.

I nodded. I listened. I absorbed the information the way you do when something feels important, but not yet fully real.

At twenty-eight, I was not actively trying to get pregnant. I was childless by choice, at least in the way that felt true at the time. I had a career that mattered to me, work that felt purposeful and grounding. I had a relationship built on love and stability. My life felt full, intentional, and largely my own. Motherhood lived somewhere ahead of me, not close enough to touch, not distant enough to ignore. I imagined it in the future, not pressing against the present.

And yet, the diagnosis reached forward and touched that future anyway. It placed uncertainty into a timeline I had quietly assumed would be there when I was ready for it.

That was the part that unraveled me.

The grief came unexpectedly and without a clear name. It was not grief for something I had lost, not exactly. It was grief for something that suddenly felt fragile. For a possibility that might now require effort, intervention, or patience I had not planned on needing. It was grief for the ease I had assumed would be mine. No one prepares you for how disorienting it is to mourn something that has not happened yet. To ache for a future that exists only as an idea, suddenly marked with a question mark.

For years, the fear had been accidental pregnancy. Late periods. Moments of panic followed by relief. Suddenly, the fear flipped. *What if I wasn't ever able to get pregnant at all?*

Fertility diagnoses carry a quiet, insidious shame. It creeps in without permission, asking questions you would never aim at another woman. *Did I wait too long? Did I push my body too hard? Did I make the wrong choices? Is this my fault?* It is astonishing how quickly compassion dissolves when things become personal, when your body feels like it has broken an unspoken promise.

I tried to outwork the uncertainty.

Fertility diagnoses alter how a woman holds hope, control, and expectation. They turn the future into a moving target and leave you standing in the present with nothing solid to hold on to. When your body stops following predictable rules, information becomes hope and action becomes reassurance.

If you are doing something, researching something, adjusting something, then maybe you are not powerless after all.

So I researched relentlessly. Podcasts played in the background during my commute, voices promising balance, healing, regulation, and answers. Articles were bookmarked and reread late into the night, my thumb scrolling while my mind raced. Supplements lined my counter like small, hopeful negotiations with my body. Inositol. Maca root. Seed cycling. Magnesium. Each one felt like a quiet bargain: *If I do this, maybe things will fall into place.* Every recommendation carried urgency, and every recommendation contradicted the one before it. Eat fewer carbohydrates. Eat more complex carbohydrates. Exercise gently. Exercise intensely. Reduce stress. Balance hormones. Support ovulation. It was dizzying, but stopping felt worse. My browser history became a record of someone trying desperately to earn certainty through effort.

Because doing nothing felt unbearable. Waiting felt dangerous. Stillness felt like giving up. And no one tells you how much shame creeps in when your body does not behave the way you were taught it is supposed to. Research becomes a way to stay hopeful without admitting how afraid you are. It becomes a way to feel responsible instead of helpless, informed instead of vulnerable.

I tracked everything. Basal body temperature. Symptoms that may or may not have meant anything at all. I watched charts rise and fall without pattern or explanation. I logged data obsessively, searching for meaning in numbers that refused to cooperate. I built spreadsheets, because structure has always been my language of safety. If I could see it laid out clearly, maybe it would make sense. Maybe my body would respond to being understood. Maybe predictability would follow effort.

But it never did.

PCOS does not respond to force. It does not reward discipline with certainty. It does not bend to planning or obedience. The harder I tried, the more obvious it became that control was an illusion. Eventually, I had to sit with the truth that my body would not be commanded into predictability. I could support it. I could nourish it. I could listen more carefully than I ever had before. But I could not manage it into submission.

That realization landed with devastation and relief intertwined. Devastation in acknowledging how little control I actually had. Relief in understanding that it was never a failure of effort. My body was not resisting me. It was communicating in the only way it knew how. And learning to listen, rather than override it, became the hardest and most honest work of all.

And still, hope remained.

It just changed shape.

Hope became quieter, more careful. It was no longer assumed. It was chosen. Held with intention instead of entitlement. Hope after uncertainty is not loud or carefree. It does not demand outcomes. It learns how to live alongside doubt. It looks like imagining a future without insisting on guarantees. It looks like holding space for possibility while accepting the unknown.

That was the beginning of a different kind of becoming.

PCOS reshaped how I saw my body, my timeline, and my sense of self. It forced me to confront how deeply I wanted motherhood, not as a milestone, but as something woven into me. Even without certainty. Even without promises.

I learned how to sit without knowing. How to advocate for myself. How to hold hope and grief at the same time without letting either consume me. The diagnosis did not define me, but it changed me. It taught me that resilience is not about certainty. It is about continuing forward even when the ground feels unstable.

My story was still unfolding. Even if the pages ahead were unclear.

For the Mama in It Right Now:
If your path includes waiting rooms, calendars marked in pencil, lab slips folded into purses, or the quiet ache of not knowing what comes next, your heart is carrying more than most people ever realize. The effort may be invisible to the outside world, but it is real. Every appointment kept, every test taken, every calculation made in the privacy of your own thoughts is an act of courage, even when it feels exhausting instead of hopeful.

If your story is lined with negative tests, unpredictable cycles, and the long stretch of waiting, please hear this clearly: you are not broken. Your body is not betraying you. It is responding as best it can with the information, care, and support it has been given. The frustration, grief, anger, and longing you feel are not personal failures. They are evidence of how deeply you care about something that matters.

You are allowed to live inside the contradictions. You can hold hope and heartbreak at the same time. You can love the life you have while mourning the one you are still reaching for. Gratitude does not erase grief, and grief does not cancel belief. These feelings often sit side by side, learning how to coexist in the same breath.

If this season feels isolating, if it seems like everyone else is moving forward while you remain suspended in uncertainty, know that you are not alone in this, even when it feels unbearably quiet. There are countless women walking similar paths, carrying the same questions, learning strength they never asked for.

You are not falling behind. You are not failing. You are becoming. Becoming more attuned to your body, more honest with your heart, more resilient than you ever expected to be. And even on the days when the waiting feels heavy and unending, that becoming still matters.

What I Wish I Knew Then:

- Hope and heartbreak often exist together.
- Your worth is not defined by cycles, hormones, or timing.
- There is no shame in wanting something deeply.
- Your path to motherhood is still your path, even if it looks different than you imagined.

3

Letting Go of the Plan

There is a story many of us are taught about how a life is supposed to unfold.

You fall in love. You get engaged. You plan a wedding. You build a home. And only then, when everything is properly arranged and publicly affirmed, you bring a child into it. The order matters, we are told. The structure matters. Follow it correctly, and life will be steadier. Easier. More acceptable. Following the sequence is supposed to protect you, to keep chaos at bay, to spare you judgment and grant you a sense of legitimacy.

I believed that story for a long time. It was the only one I had ever been offered.

I was raised Catholic, surrounded by traditions that shaped not just faith, but expectation. Marriage came first. Children followed. That sequence was framed as moral and practical, a foundation strong enough to carry everything else. It was spoken as wisdom, not preference. As truth, not suggestion. I absorbed it quietly, the way we absorb most inherited beliefs, without ever stopping to consider whether it would fit the life

I would one day live.

For years, that imagined order felt distant enough not to question. There was time, I assumed. Time to establish a career first. Time to meet milestones in the proper order, without rush or disruption. The future felt generous, patient, and available.

Then PCOS entered the picture, and that story began to loosen at the seams.

The diagnosis did not arrive with urgency or panic. It did not demand immediate decisions or dramatic shifts. Instead, it brought a quiet recalibration. A subtle but unmistakable change in how I understood time. Suddenly, the future felt less accommodating. Less guaranteed. The timeline I had always assumed would be waiting for me now felt conditional, as though it might move forward without me if I waited too long to step into it.

I began to feel the tension between the life I had been taught to plan and the life my body might require me to choose.

I had imagined my life unfolding in a specific order. Love, then marriage, then motherhood. That order felt safe. Familiar. Approved. It was the version of adulthood that received nods of encouragement instead of raised eyebrows. The version that allowed you to move through the world without having to explain yourself or justify your choices.

But sitting with a fertility-impacting diagnosis forced me to confront a question I had never expected to ask so soon, or so honestly.

What if waiting came at a cost?

What if following the "right" order meant risking the very thing I had always assumed would come easily when the time was right? What if the structure I had been taught to trust was not built with diagnoses like mine in mind? What if the story I had believed so

27

deeply was never meant to be universal, but simply traditional?

Those questions did not arrive with clear answers. They arrived with discomfort. With grief. With a quiet unraveling of assumptions I did not realize I had built my future on.

And in that unraveling, I began to understand that becoming a mother might require me to release not just fear, but expectation. Not just uncertainty, but permission. Permission to imagine a life that did not follow the script, but still held meaning, love, and legitimacy.

That realization did not make the path clearer. But it made it more honest.

And, I was learning, that mattered more than order ever could.

There comes a moment for many women when the story they were handed no longer fits the life they are living. It does not always arrive dramatically. Sometimes it comes quietly, through a choice that feels right but looks wrong from the outside. Sometimes it arrives through timing that cannot be controlled, through love that deepens faster than expected, through loss or surprise or longing that does not wait for permission. Motherhood has a way of exposing how rigid those inherited timelines really are. How little room they leave for bodies that do not cooperate, relationships that evolve differently, or lives that refuse to follow a single approved order. And in that realization, many of us are forced to ask not what we were taught to want, but what we actually need.

For every mother, there is a reckoning with expectation. With the quiet pressure to justify your choices, to explain your timing, to reassure others that your life still makes sense to them. Whether you became a mother sooner than planned, later than expected, through loss, through assistance, through surprise, or after years of waiting, there is often a moment when you realize that no version of motherhood comes without questions. No path arrives without commentary. And yet, what matters most is rarely visible to anyone else. It lives in the way you show up. In the way you choose love over fear. In the way you build safety and belonging, even when the blueprint you were given does not apply. Motherhood is not validated by sequence. It is validated by presence. By intention. By the quiet, daily decision to choose your child and the life you are creating, again and again.

I did not want to rush marriage. Not because I doubted love, but because I respected it too much to let fear be the driving force. I wanted a commitment that was entered with intention, not urgency. One chosen because it felt steady and right, not because a diagnosis had introduced a countdown I could hear ticking in the background. I wanted marriage to come from joy, from mutual readiness, from the kind of certainty that grows slowly and roots itself deeply. I did not want the most meaningful promises of my life shaped by pressure, even pressure that came disguised as practicality.

There is a particular kind of grief in realizing that two things you value deeply may not move at the same pace. I wanted to honor the relationship we were building without allowing anxiety about the future to distort it. I wanted our commitment to be something we ran toward, not something we rushed into because we were afraid of what might happen if we waited. Love, I believed, deserved patience. It deserved space. It deserved to be chosen freely, not cornered by circumstance.

And yet, motherhood was no longer something I could tuck neatly into a distant chapter of my life. It was no longer an abstract someday or a vague intention. It felt present in a way that surprised me. Not loud or frantic, but insistent. Like something tapping gently at the edge of my awareness, asking to be acknowledged. It was difficult to explain without sounding dramatic, without inviting misunderstanding. It wasn't panic. It wasn't desperation. It was clarity.

A quiet understanding had settled in me that time might not behave the way I had always trusted it would. That waiting, while still valid, now carried weight. That the future was not something I could assume would pause politely until every piece of my life was arranged just so. I could still move thoughtfully. I could still choose intentionally. But I could no longer pretend that timing was entirely flexible or infinite.

I found myself holding two truths at once. I could honor love without rushing it. And I could honor my longing for motherhood without denying it. Neither desire canceled the other out. They simply asked more of me than I had expected. More honesty. More courage. More willingness to sit in the tension between what I wanted and what I could not fully control.

When I told my boyfriend about the diagnosis, I told him everything. I did not soften it or filter it. I shared the uncertainty, the statistics that refused to land cleanly, the vague language doctors use when outcomes cannot be promised. I told him what PCOS could mean. That cycles might remain irregular. That ovulation might be unpredictable. That fertility, for some women, becomes more complicated with time. That waiting, while still possible, could make things harder, not easier. I wanted him to understand the reality, not just the hope.

I also told him about what might come next if conception was not simple. The appointments that can start to feel endless.

The monitoring. The medications that alter moods and expectations. The monthly rhythm of hope and disappointment that can strain even the strongest relationships. We talked about how infertility can quietly insert itself into a partnership, turning intimacy into scheduling, turning tenderness into pressure, turning love into something measured in cycles and outcomes. I knew how easily it could exhaust communication, test patience, and magnify fears neither partner knew they were carrying.

And then I told him something else, something that took more courage to say than the diagnosis itself. I told him he did not have to stay. That if this was not the life he wanted, if the unknowns felt like too much, he was allowed to choose differently. I needed his choice to be free, not tethered by obligation or guilt. I needed to know that if he stayed, it would be with eyes open and heart willing. Not just for a baby, but for the emotional terrain we might have to cross to get there.

He did not hesitate.

He took my hand, steady and certain, and said we would face whatever came next together. Not if things worked out. Not only if it was easy. Whatever came. There was no bargaining in his voice, no pause while he calculated the cost. Just a calm, grounded commitment that settled something deep inside me. In that moment, fear loosened its grip. I was no longer carrying the weight of the unknown alone.

Throughout the process, he was unwavering. He listened when I spiraled and did not try to fix what could not be fixed. He learned alongside me. He made room for my grief without taking it personally. He made room for my fear without retreating. His presence made the uncertainty survivable.

That was when I learned something important about commitment. Sometimes it does not begin with a ring or a ceremony or a perfectly timed proposal. Sometimes it begins in an ordinary room, on an ordinary night, when two people decide to carry something heavy side by side. When love shows up not as grand promises, but as quiet resolve.

Choosing to try for a baby before marriage was not impulsive. It was deeply considered. It came after long conversations that stretched late into the night, after honest reckoning with fear, timing, faith, and reality. It came from understanding that PCOS does not wait politely for life to feel perfectly arranged. That fertility does not always align with tradition or expectation. That sometimes you have to respond to the body you are in, not the story you were taught.

This was not a rejection of commitment. It was a form of it.

We were choosing each other in the middle of uncertainty. Choosing to protect our relationship even as we stepped into unknown territory. Choosing to move forward with intention rather than fear. Choosing to build something real, even if it did not follow the order we once imagined. And in that choice, I felt more secure than any timeline or tradition could have ever made me feel.

Still, the opinions came.

They were rarely loud. Rarely confrontational. No one stood in front of me and told me I was making the wrong choice. Instead, the opinions arrived sideways, wrapped in careful language and good intentions. They showed up as pauses that lingered a second too long. As questions asked gently, but with an edge of concern just beneath the surface.

Family opinions carry a particular weight. These are the voices that shape your earliest understanding of right and wrong. When their expectations shift, even subtly, you feel it not just emotionally, but physically. In your chest. In your stomach. In the instinctive urge to explain yourself before anyone has even asked.

I could feel their quiet reassessment of the order I was choosing. The gentle surprise that I was stepping outside the structure I had been raised to value. No one said disappointment out loud, but I felt the pressure to justify. To reassure. To prove that I had thought this through. That I was not being reckless. That I was still responsible. Still grounded. Still worthy of approval.

I wanted to honor them. I wanted to make them proud. I wanted them to see that the values they had instilled in me had not disappeared simply because my life was unfolding differently than expected. At the same time, I needed to honor myself. The woman I had become. The information I now had. The reality of my body and my future. Holding both of those desires at once felt like standing in the middle of a quiet tug of war, pulled by love in two directions.

That tension lived inside me, persistent and exhausting. It asked me, again and again, to choose between comfort and honesty. Between following a script that would make everyone else feel comfortable and listening to the clarity that had settled into my own heart. I questioned myself constantly, replaying conversations in my head long after they ended. Reading into tone. Interpreting silence. Wondering whether I was disappointing the people who mattered most to me.

Was I acting from fear or from clarity?

Was this decision rooted in anxiety, or in truth?

Was I betraying the values I was raised with, or finally applying them with discernment and maturity?

Those questions did not come with easy answers. They

required me to sit with discomfort instead of rushing to resolve it. To accept that doing what was right for me might still cause unease for others.

Choosing differently did not mean rejecting my upbringing. It meant honoring its deeper intention. I was choosing responsibility, commitment, and love, just not in the order I had been taught to expect. And learning to hold that truth, even when it was misunderstood, became one of the earliest lessons of motherhood, long before I ever held my child.

More than the opinions of others, more than the raised eyebrows or careful silences, I worried about the child I hoped for.

I worried about how timelines get interpreted long after the details fade. I worried that one day she might look at the order of our lives and wonder what it meant about her place in it. I worried she might ask herself whether she had been wanted or simply accommodated.

That fear lodged itself deeper than any judgment from the outside world ever could.

I wanted her to know, without hesitation or doubt, that she was never an accident. Never a compromise. Never the result of panic or pressure. I wanted her to know that she was hoped for deliberately, held in our minds and hearts long before she arrived. That her life was not born out of urgency, but out of trust. Trust in love. Trust in timing that did not follow the rules we were given. Trust that choosing her, even before we met her, was the right and very best decision we had ever made. I wanted her to grow up rooted in the certainty that she was chosen.

What I did not want her to know was how much I cried in the months after my diagnosis. How often the negative tests left me staring at my own reflection, wondering why my body felt like it was working against me instead of with me. I did not want her to know how many times I sat with disappointment that had nowhere to land, the quiet devastation of cycles that ended before they ever truly began. The waiting. The tracking. The way hope would rise only to come crashing down with each negative pregnancy test.

There were nights when my thoughts drifted further ahead, beyond pregnancy, beyond infancy, into futures I could not yet see clearly. I thought about what I might pass on to her. PCOS has a way of threading itself quietly through generations, showing up without warning, passed from mothers to daughters. The thought that my daughter might one day sit where I had sat, staring at a test, questioning her body, questioning herself, and her worth cracked something open in me.

I imagined her wondering if her dreams were asking too much of her body. If patience would ever be enough.

That possibility hurt in a way I was not prepared for. I wish, fiercely, that her path will be easier. That her body would cooperate without resistance. That she would never doubt her worth because of hormones, timelines, or test results. I want her to move through her life without that ache. I want her to know ease.

And then, slowly, another truth settled in.

If she did inherit my challenges, she might also inherit my resilience.

She might inherit the ability to sit with uncertainty without collapsing under it. The courage to advocate for her body. The capacity to hope carefully, intentionally, without surrendering to despair. She might inherit the knowledge that her worth has never been measured by what her body does or does not do. She might inherit the strength to ask for help, to adjust expectations, to build a life that fits her reality rather than the story she was handed.

She might inherit a mother who teaches her, through example, that becoming is not linear and that love is not conditional on ease.

And in that realization, my fear softened into something else. Not certainty. Not peace. But resolve.

Whatever her path one day looks like, she will not walk it alone. She will not have to wonder whether she was wanted. She will not have to earn her place. She will grow up knowing that her life was chosen with care, held with reverence, and loved long before it ever took shape.

That, more than anything, is what I want to give her.

Choosing to try for our child before marriage was not easy. It required sitting with discomfort, with disappointment, with the possibility of misunderstanding. But it also brought clarity. It taught me that commitment is not defined by sequence. It is defined by presence. By showing up. By choosing love even when it does not fit neatly into expectation.

And that choice, imperfect and deeply human, shaped the mother I was becoming.

For the Mama in It Right Now:

If your path to motherhood does not follow the timeline you imagined or the order you were taught to expect, give yourself grace. There is no single right way to build a family. There is only the way that fits your life, your values, and the truth you are standing in.

If you feel the weight of others' opinions pressing in on your decisions, know that their discomfort does not mean you are doing something wrong. Family pressure, cultural expectations, and deeply rooted traditions can make even the most thoughtful choices feel heavy. It is okay to honor where you come from while still choosing differently for where you are going.

If you find yourself questioning whether you are being brave or fearful, intentional or reactive, remember this: thoughtful decisions are rarely free of doubt. Love-led choices often come with uncertainty. That does not make them reckless. It makes them human.

If you worry about how your future child might one day interpret your story, know that children feel intention long before they understand timelines. They feel love in the way they are spoken about, hoped for, and held. Your desire to protect them from confusion or pain already reflects the depth of your care.

You do not owe anyone an explanation for your life. The order of events does not determine the strength of the family you build. Commitment is not only marked by ceremonies or milestones. It is lived in the quiet, daily choosing of one another, especially when the path forward is uncertain.

Your story is yours. And it is worthy of trust, respect, and compassion, especially from yourself.

What I Wish I Knew Then:

- There's no single "right way" to build a family, only *your* way.
- The opinions of others fade; the love you nurture endures.
- You don't have to defend your story. It speaks for itself.

4

Pregnant, Sort of Prepared

When I finally saw a positive pregnancy test, it didn't arrive the way I had imagined it would.

There was no dramatic pause. No gasp. No moment where the world fell silent and rearranged itself around the news. Instead, it arrived quietly. Almost unreal. Like something fragile that did not yet trust me to hold it.

I stared at the faint pink lines for a long time, afraid that looking too closely might undo it. Afraid that believing too quickly would invite disappointment back in. Joy hovered just out of reach, restrained by months of learning how to brace myself.

After months of negative tests, hope had learned to be careful. It had learned to lower its voice. With PCOS, nothing felt reliable. A late period was not a promise. Nausea was not reassurance. Tenderness, fatigue, hunger, none of it meant what I wanted it to mean. My body had taught me not to read into signals, not to trust symptoms, not to assume anything. I had learned to keep my expectations small and my emotions guarded, to protect myself from the quiet devastation that came with getting it wrong.

So when that second line appeared, faint but undeniable, my instinct was not celebration. It was disbelief.

I questioned the lighting. The angle. The test itself. I held it closer, then farther away, as if distance might clarify whether this was real or just another trick of timing and hormones. I told myself not to react yet. Not to name it. Not to let it settle into my body before I knew it would stay.

Disbelief felt safer than joy. Disbelief did not ask me to risk my heart again.

I was so unsure of what I was seeing that I took a picture and sent it to a friend, not to announce anything, but to ask a question. *Is this real? Do you see it too?* I needed someone outside my own fear to tell me whether the line was actually there or whether my longing had finally learned how to hallucinate.

That moment holds so much of what this journey required from the people who loved me. I am forever grateful for the friends who sat with me through the waiting and the wondering. Friends who never minimized the grief of negative tests or tried to rush me into optimism. Friends who reminded me, again and again, that my body was not broken, that my worth was not measured by cycles or timing, that I was still whole even when things felt uncertain.

That friend, especially, held hope for me when I could not hold it for myself. She looked at that photo and saw clearly what I could not yet trust. *"Yes"*, she said. *"It is positive."* And in that confirmation, something inside me finally softened enough to begin letting the truth in.

The emotional whiplash came all at once. Shock. Fear. Gratitude. A kind of joy that felt too big to hold. And underneath it all, a single steady thought: *This is happening.*

For the first time, hope had somewhere to land.

And in that moment, I realized how much I had endured to get here. How many times I had asked my heart to quiet itself. How carefully I had learned to want. That tiny line carried more weight than I was prepared for, not because it promised certainty, but because it proved possibility.

My boyfriend was working out of town and wasn't expected home for another two days. The timing felt cruel in a way I couldn't quite articulate. This was not news meant to be carried alone. It felt too fragile and too enormous all at the same time. I moved through the day in a fog, answering emails, making small talk, pretending the world had not fundamentally shifted beneath my feet.

That night, unexpectedly, he came home early.

I didn't know what to do with the sudden rush of relief. I waited up, restless and wired, pacing between the couch and the window, my thoughts looping. When I heard the door open around eleven o'clock, my heart leapt before my mind could catch up. Our black lab greeted him first, tail wagging wildly. I had tied a small note to his collar, hands trembling as I did it.

"Guess what?" it read.

My boyfriend bent down, unhooked the note, and unfolded it slowly. I watched his face change in real time, confusion giving way to disbelief, disbelief softening into something like awe.

"Mom's pregnant."

For a moment, he just stared at me. Then at the note. Then back at me, as if he needed to see it written again to believe it. The room felt suddenly full. Full of relief I hadn't realized I was carrying. Full of gratitude. Full of overwhelming happiness.

Even in that moment, fear lingered.

Pregnancy after uncertainty does not arrive cleanly wrapped

in joy. It comes layered with caution learned the hard way. When hope has been fragile for so long, your body learns restraint before your heart has a chance to catch up. I wanted to believe fully, to let excitement rush in without hesitation, but something in me held back. I had learned not to trust joy too quickly. Not because I was ungrateful, but because I was protective.

Each twinge in my body became a question mark. *Was that normal? Was that something? Was it nothing at all?* Symptoms felt unreliable. My body had spent months teaching me not to assume, not to expect, not to celebrate too early. And even now, with proof in my hands, that lesson lingered.

The first weeks became consumed by preparation, not because I believed preparation could guarantee safety, but because it gave my hands something to do while my heart tried to catch up. Research became a form of love. I read obsessively. Lists of foods to avoid. Guidelines for what was safe and what was suddenly off-limits. Registries that felt overwhelming and oddly comforting at the same time. Apps that measured our baby in fruit sizes and described, week by week, the invisible work happening inside my body. I bookmarked nursery ideas, prenatal checklists, labor tips, anything that made this feel tangible.

Every small decision carried a weight it never had before. What I ate. How I slept. How I moved through the world. Pregnancy quietly rearranges your priorities before anyone else can see it happening. Your body is no longer just yours. Your choices ripple outward in ways you can feel but not yet see.

And still, no amount of preparation made me feel ready.

That is one of the first truths pregnancy teaches you, whether you are prepared to hear it or not. Readiness is not a destination you arrive at. It is not something you earn through enough research, enough planning, or enough reassurance from people who have done this before. You do not wake up one morning and suddenly feel equipped for the magnitude of what is coming. Readiness, I learned, is something you practice. Quietly. Imperfectly. In the small, unseen decisions that begin to shape your days long before anyone else knows they matter.

Those early weeks, when only the two of us knew, felt sacred in a way I had not expected. It was like carrying a truth that hummed just beneath the surface of ordinary life, steady and alive. We moved through grocery stores and late dinners and long drives with this invisible knowing between us, touching it gently, almost reverently, as if checking in on something fragile and miraculous at the same time. Sometimes it was a glance held a second too long. Sometimes it was a hand finding mine without explanation. Sometimes it was nothing more than a shared breath, a quiet acknowledgment that everything had already shifted.

There was tenderness in that privacy. A softness I would later miss. It felt protective, as if the joy needed time to root itself before being shared with the world. Before opinions. Before questions. Before other people's fears or expectations had a chance to seep in. We were scared, of course. How could we not be? But excitement pulsed beneath everything, steady and insistent, refusing to be ignored. Even the mundane felt altered. Conversations carried new meaning. Silence felt full instead of empty. The world had not changed, but the way I moved through it had. It was as if everything had tilted slightly, just enough to make room for something new to begin taking shape.

Those weeks were not loud or celebratory. They were

quiet, cautious, deeply intimate. And in that quiet, I was already learning something essential about motherhood. That it requires holding fear and hope in the same hands. That joy does not need certainty to be real. That you can love something fiercely while still being afraid of how much there is to lose. I was learning how to step forward without guarantees, how to make space for what was unfolding without trying to control it.

The physical changes came quickly.

Exhaustion settled into my body in a way I had never known. This was not tiredness that could be fixed with sleep or a slower weekend. It was depleting. A full-body heaviness that made even rest feel incomplete. My body felt unfamiliar, sensitive, and fragile all at once. I had spent years carrying emotional weight through my work, but this was different. This responsibility was not theoretical. It lived inside me. It could not be set down or shared or deferred. It demanded presence at all times, whether I felt capable of giving it or not.

Doctor's appointments brought relief and renewed anxiety in equal measure. Each heartbeat steadied me. Each pause, each moment of waiting, unsettled me. I learned quickly that you can follow every recommendation, do everything "right," and still feel exposed. Pregnancy does not reward perfection with certainty. You can be careful and afraid at the same time. You can be grateful and overwhelmed in the same breath.

By the second trimester, the fog lifted slightly. Energy returned in small, uneven waves. And then there was movement. Tiny flutters at first, so subtle I questioned whether they were real. Gas or muscle or imagination. And then, unmistakable kicks. Each one anchored me to the truth that this life, so long imagined and cautiously hoped for, was real. My protectiveness sharpened. My awareness widened. I began moving through the world with a different kind of care.

The second trimester brought tangibility. Registries. Classes. Conversations that no longer felt hypothetical. I adjusted routines and made choices I had never considered before. How I nourished a body that was no longer just mine. Motherhood revealed itself slowly, not in grand moments, but in vigilance and surrender. In learning when to plan and when to let go. In realizing that control was never part of the agreement.

My identity stretched.

People noticed the bump. They offered congratulations. Many shared advice, some helpful, and some unsolicited. Emotionally, I discovered depths I had not known existed. The instinct to protect was no longer abstract or aspirational. It lived in my body. It showed up in how I scanned rooms, how I listened differently, how I felt the world more acutely than before.

By the third trimester, everything felt heavier. My body grew unfamiliar yet miraculous. Sleep became elusive. Discomfort constant. Fear and awe often collided within the same hour. I worried about labor and my ability to endure. I worried about my capacity to protect this life once it existed outside of me. There were unknowns no checklist could prepare me for, no advice could fully ease.

And yet, clarity emerged.

Motherhood was not asking me to be perfect. It was asking me to be present. To show up even when I was unsure. To choose another life quietly and fiercely, again and again, without needing to feel ready first.

As the due date approached, anticipation and vigilance fused into a single truth. I would never be fully prepared. Birth, like motherhood itself, does not wait for certainty. Preparation can guide you, but it cannot shield you from vulnerability. And vulnerability, I was learning, was not a sign of weakness. It was part of the passage.

And still, there was peace.

I had grown into this role without realizing it. Every adjustment, every choice, every conversation had been practice. I was no longer preparing for motherhood. I was living it.

I waited not without fear, but with openness. Holding hope and uncertainty in the same hand. Trusting that becoming a mother was not about having it all figured out, but about stepping forward anyway.

For the Mama in It Right Now:

If you are newly pregnant and find yourself holding joy and fear at the same time, you are not doing it wrong. You are responding honestly to something that matters deeply. Pregnancy does not arrive as a single emotion. It arrives layered. You can feel grateful and terrified. You can feel excited and cautious. You can love this life fiercely while still wondering if your heart is strong enough to hold all the unknowns that come with it.

If you are waiting for the moment when you finally feel "ready," when the fear quiets and confidence takes its place, know that many mothers never experience that shift in the way they expect. Readiness doesn't always arrive as certainty. Often, it shows up as care. As vigilance. As the quiet way you think twice about everything now, because someone else is suddenly at the center of your world.

If your excitement feels fragile, if you guard your hope carefully, especially after loss, infertility, or uncertainty, that does not make you ungrateful. It makes you wise. Protecting your heart is a form of love, too. You are allowed to celebrate cautiously. You are allowed to wait before you share the news. You are allowed to feel connected and detached in the same breath.

If you find yourself researching everything and still feeling unprepared, know this: no amount of information will fully quiet the vulnerability that comes with carrying a life. Preparation can guide you, but it cannot eliminate uncertainty. That doesn't mean you are failing. It means you are stepping into something that cannot be mastered, only experienced.

And if some days you feel strong and capable, while others you feel overwhelmed and unsure, remember that both can coexist. Motherhood begins long before birth, and it begins not with confidence, but with presence. With choosing to show up again and again, even when fear whispers loudly.

You do not need to have it all figured out. You do not need to feel brave every day. The fact that you care this deeply already tells the story of the kind of mother you are becoming.

What I Wish I Knew Then:

- Fear does not mean something is wrong. It means something matters.
- You don't need to know how to be a mother before you are one.
- Preparation is helpful, but presence is transformative.
- Your intuition will grow louder than your doubt.

5

Strength Looks Different Here

They tell you not to make a birth plan because babies do not read, but most expecting mothers still write one. It feels instinctual, because when you are pregnant, planning can feel like the only thing you can hold onto. I imagined a calm room, dim lights, my boyfriend's hand in mine, and a quiet, steady entrance into motherhood. I wanted peace, or at least a sense of intentionality. Instead, what unfolded was something far more complicated, something that would shape how I understood myself as a mother long before I ever held my daughter.

It was three in the morning when I woke up, which was not unusual. At thirty-eight weeks pregnant, I was not really sleeping anymore so much as drifting in and out of uncomfortable half-naps between bathroom trips and the baby practicing gymnastics on my ribs. This night felt no different. Just another bleary-eyed shuffle toward the bathroom, until it wasn't. As I stood up, a sudden warmth slid down my legs. I froze. Another drip. Then another. A wetness I could not stop, no matter how hard I tried.

For one disorienting second, time stopped.

Was this my water breaking, or had I actually peed myself?

That is the humbling thing about the end of pregnancy. Your body stops asking for permission. It becomes its own unpredictable universe. Sitting on the edge of the bed at three in the morning, I realized motherhood might begin with the most confusing question imaginable.

I shook my boyfriend awake and told him what was happening. My voice sounded half panicked, half disbelieving when I said, "I'm ninety-five percent sure my water just broke."

His squinting, half-asleep response, something we still laugh about, was, "Are you sure you didn't just pee?"

Pregnancy humbles you, but this was a new level.

What makes moments like this universal is that almost every mother has some version of this bewildering beginning. A moment where excitement, panic, denial, humor, and bodily mystery collide in a way nothing else in life prepares you for. Whether water breaks in a dramatic movie-worthy gush, in a confusing trickle like mine, or not at all, every mother knows the emotional whiplash of standing at the threshold of labor thinking, *Is this it? Am I imagining this? Am I supposed to know what's happening? Why does no one prepare you for the uncertainty?*

Those first minutes felt like a reflection of the entire pregnancy. The constant mental loop of: *Is this happening? Am I ready? Is my body doing what it's supposed to do?*

Even with all those questions swirling, we made the strangest decision. My boyfriend and I both went to work that morning. Looking back, it was not logic guiding us. It was denial disguised as normalcy. It was the mind clinging to routine because routine felt safer than acknowledging that life as we knew it was tipping into something entirely new. There is something deeply human about trying to squeeze in one more ordinary morning before everything changes forever.

It helped that my office sat right next door to the hospital where we planned to deliver. That proximity felt like a safety net. If things escalated quickly, help was literally steps away. So we pretended nothing extraordinary was beginning. We got dressed. We grabbed our bags. We moved through the motions while the biggest moment of our lives quietly unfolded beneath the surface.

Looking back now, I see how relatable that morning was. How many mothers have lived some version of that same blurry, bewildering start. The moment when logic meets instinct, when excitement collides with fear, when your world is about to split open in the most beautiful way and you are still trying to decide if you just peed yourself.

Labor rarely begins the way you expect. But it begins. Messy, confusing, humbling, and somehow entirely perfect in its own chaotic way.

By late morning, the contractions were no longer subtle. They had shifted from light tightenings I could ignore to a steady rhythm that demanded attention. We finally decided it was time to head to the hospital. Walking through those doors felt surreal, like stepping into the moment every book, every appointment, every late-night worry had been preparing me for. I felt nervous, hopeful, and braced for answers.

A nurse swabbed me and confirmed what I already suspected. My water had broken. There was relief in that validation, proof that I had not imagined it, proof that something real was happening. But then everything sped up in a way that did not feel like mine. The nurse stepped out to consult the doctor, who never came into the room, never laid eyes on me, never asked a single question, yet ordered that I be admitted and immediately placed on Pitocin.

The shift was jarring. One moment I was being assessed, the next decisions were being made about me without being made with me. The pressure rose quickly. There was an unspoken message that I needed to comply, to move along, to fit neatly into the system's timeline. But inside, my body did not feel ready. My instincts did not align with the urgency filling the room.

So I asked for a cervical check. I needed something concrete, something that could tell me whether my body was actually keeping pace with the momentum around me.

"You're two centimeters," the nurse said.

Two centimeters.

It felt like the most discouraging number in the world.

Every labor story has a moment like this. A moment when the numbers do not match the effort, when progress feels invisible, when your body becomes a measurement instead of a miracle. Hearing "two centimeters" made me feel behind before I had even begun. Like my body was failing an exam I did not know how to study for.

Standing there in a thin gown under fluorescent lights, clarity rose in me. Not defiance, but certainty. I was not ready to hand over my experience. I was not ready to abandon the birth I had envisioned, the one that felt right in my heart. So I waited. I listened to my body. And I chose to leave.

Against medical advice.

Against the momentum of the room.

Against the pressure to be a "good patient."

For some women, reclaiming birth looks like advocating loudly. For others, it looks like surrendering fully to intervention. For me, in that moment, it looked like choosing myself.

Birth asks every mother, in one way or another, to make peace with the tension between trust and control. There is no single right way to do that. There is only the way that allows you to stay connected to yourself in the midst of something that can feel consuming, overwhelming, and strangely public all at once. Leaving was not about rejecting care. It was about remembering that I was not just a body being managed. I was a person becoming a mother.

Those hours at home were grounding in ways I did not yet understand I would need. Without machines, bright lights, or constant interruptions, labor felt different. Safer. I could move how my body wanted to move. I could breathe without explanation. I could lean, sway, collapse, and gather myself again without being asked to quantify pain. Time loosened. I was no longer watching the clock or waiting for permission. I was inside myself, meeting each contraction as it came, learning in real time what it meant to endure something you cannot escape, only move through.

For a little while, labor felt sacred. Not because it was easy, it wasn't. But because I felt present. And that presence mattered. Birth, I would learn, is not defined by how it unfolds on paper. It is defined by whether you feel seen, supported, and allowed to inhabit your body fully, whatever choices that requires. Some mothers find that in hospitals. Some find it in birth centers, or operating rooms, or quiet bedrooms at home. What matters is not the setting, but the empowerment. The sense that, even when plans change, you are still part of the decision-making, still held in your humanity.

By late evening, the contractions deepened. They pulled me inward in that primal way only labor can. And I knew it was time to return to the hospital. Walking back through the doors felt heavier. The stakes felt higher. I was no longer choosing rest; I was choosing endurance.

And that was where everything shifted.

We were stepping into what would become a forty-five-hour labor—something I could not have imagined then, and something I could not have prepared for even if someone had warned me.

The next ten hours unfolded with a kind of grace I wish every mother could experience. My boyfriend anchored me through every contraction, learning counter pressure techniques in real time and applying them with steady focus. His hands became the place I trusted, the place I leaned into.

The room was dim. Lavender filled the air thanks to a kind and attentive nurse. She did not just monitor vitals. She saw me. She reminded me I was capable. Her voice threaded through the pain, steady and grounding. Each word of encouragement felt like a lifeline. She helped transform the room from something clinical into a space where I could own my strength.

I labored in the tub, the warm water offering brief moments of relief that made each contraction feel manageable. There is something ancient about laboring in water, the way it softens the edges, the way your body feels both heavy and buoyant at the same time.

For a while, it was everything I had hoped for.

Hard, of course.

But purposeful.

Empowering.

Every surge felt like forward motion.

Every breath felt intentional.

Every moment felt possible.

I let myself believe the plan might hold.

There was beauty woven into the pain. There was a quiet, pulsing reminder that something extraordinary was happening. And for a moment, I let myself believe I might be one of those women who births exactly the way she planned. One of those rare stories where the plan holds. Where the body cooperates. Where the universe agrees. I held onto that hope tightly, for as long as labor allowed.

But motherhood has its own sense of humor. It gives you peace before chaos and asks you to hold both.

After twenty-four hours, Pitocin was administered and it changed everything. The contractions intensified, stacking on top of one another. I clung to the bed, to my breath, to whatever strength I could still access. Labor asks for reserves you do not know you have until they are demanded.

The epidural numbed only half my body. A second epidural attempt failed. The pain continued, sharp and relentless. Hours blurred into exhaustion and fear.

By six centimeters, my body began retaining fluids and my kidneys struggled. The tone shifted again, this time toward urgency. Birth was no longer about preference. It was about safety.

I was taken for an emergency C-section. When the spinal failed, I was placed under general anesthesia. My boyfriend could not be in the room during the operation. Because of the general anesthesia, I wasn't awake for the moment our daughter entered the world and took her first breath. The vision I had carried for months, the weight of her tiny body in my arms, the warmth of her skin, the sharp, miraculous sound of her cry... it all vanished in an instant.

I woke from the anesthesia, already a mother, stitched and disoriented. There was no memory of her first cry that reached my ears, no tender warmth of skin-to-skin, no gasp of awe as I saw her tiny face for the first time. I learned about her arrival through photos a kind nurse had taken, snapshots meant to fill in the moments that the anesthesia stole. They were precious, but they were not the moments I had imagined.

Her father was brought in immediately after the c-section. I am endlessly grateful he was there. That he held her first. That he carried our love into those moments I could not be fully present for. He was there for both of us. There for me, stitched and groggy, and her, new to the world. He bridged the moments I missed, and held our little family together.

Motherhood often begins with expectation, and one of its earliest lessons is how quickly those expectations fall away. Trauma is not always loud. Sometimes it is the quiet shock of absence.

When I finally held her, I traced her face, breathed her in, and learned that motherhood does not begin with perfection. It begins with presence, even when it arrives late.

Labor taught me that motherhood is a contradiction. It is both pain and power. Fear and awe. Breaking open and becoming whole at the same time. It was chaotic and painful, yet beautiful and empowering. In one breath, I felt myself coming undone; in the next, I felt stronger than I ever had. Even at its hardest, I never wished it away. I would choose it again and again because it was the cost of meeting the tiny person I had loved long before she arrived. And that's something mothers rarely say out loud: the lengths you go to for a baby you haven't even met are astounding. The moment those two pink lines appear, life shifts. Every bite of food becomes research, every product in your home becomes a question of safety. You sacrifice sleep, comfort, spontaneity, and sometimes your sanity, because your heart chose this child before your arms ever held them.

My story was not what I planned. But it was mine.

And that was how I entered motherhood. Not gracefully. Not without fear. But fully, honestly, and with a strength I never knew I had.

For the Mama in It Right Now:

If your birth did not unfold the way you hoped or imagined, pause here for a moment. You did not fail. You did not do anything wrong. You do not need to edit your story into something softer or easier to digest. It is allowed to be complicated. You are allowed to hold grief alongside love, disappointment alongside gratitude. You survived something immense, something that demanded strength from you in ways you could not have anticipated.

Birth does not define your worth as a mother. There is no single right way to enter motherhood and no perfect version of labor that guarantees peace or confidence on the other side. What defines us instead is what we discover when the plan dissolves. The strength that surfaces when control slips away. The courage it takes to keep going through pain, fear, and uncertainty because someone else suddenly matters more than your own comfort.

If you feel shaken by how it unfolded, if parts of your story feel tender or unresolved, know that this does not mean you are ungrateful or weak. It means you are human. Trauma does not always announce itself loudly. Sometimes it arrives quietly, in the moments you missed, in the choices you did not get to make, and in the version of the experience you had to let go of.

You brought life into the world through endurance you did

not know you possessed. Through surrender. Through bravery that did not look like what you expected. That strength still lives in you, even if you cannot fully name it yet. And it will continue to shape the mother you are becoming, not because of how birth looked, but because of how deeply you showed up when it mattered most.

What I Wish I Knew Then:

- Your birth story is not a reflection of your worth, your capability, or your love as a mother.
- You are allowed to grieve the experience you hoped for, even as you cherish the child you hold. Those truths can exist together.
- Strength is not measured by how birth appeared from the outside, but by how you endured, adapted, and kept going when the ground shifted beneath you.
- Healing does not follow a timeline. Emotional healing and physical healing often move at different paces, and both deserve patience, compassion, and care.
- You do not need to rush toward acceptance. Understanding and peace come slowly, and they arrive in their own time.

6

The Fourth Trimester

No one tells you that after birth, you are not finished becoming.

They tell you about the baby. About feeding schedules and sleep deprivation and how many diapers you will go through in a single day. They talk about milestones and growth charts and what to expect in those early weeks. What they do not always tell you is that you, too, are in a fragile state. That while a baby is being born into the world, a mother is being born alongside her.

The fourth trimester is not just about recovery. It is about transformation.

The name itself feels misleading. "Fourth trimester" sounds soft, almost gentle, as if it implies continuity. As if pregnancy simply extends forward, just on the outside now. But the reality is far more disorienting. I remember sitting on the couch in the early days, my baby asleep on my chest, the television muted, the house still. I was never alone, and yet I had never felt more isolated. I was needed constantly, urgently, and still parts of me felt unseen. My presence was required, but my identity felt quieter, dimmed by the sheer volume of care I was giving.

57

The days and nights lost their shape quickly. I remember staring at the clock at 3:17 a.m., its blue numbers glowing too brightly in the dark, trying to decide whether it was still night or already morning. My baby's breath was warm against my skin. The rest of the house stayed impossibly quiet. Time no longer moved in predictable units. Hours blurred together until the clock became more of a suggestion than a guide.

I stopped measuring time by mornings and evenings and began measuring it by feedings. By diaper changes. By stretches of sleep that felt both precious and insufficient. The world narrowed to a small, repetitive loop of tending and soothing, of holding and setting her down, of picking her back up when the last attempt didn't work.

My body, still healing, moved carefully through these routines. I learned how to shift her weight from one arm to the other without pulling at sore muscles. How to stand up slowly from the couch, bracing myself before moving.

Sleep came in fragments. Basic needs became negotiable. Showering felt like a small victory. The baby swing in the bathroom became my quiet savior. It allowed me to shower and get ready while keeping her close enough to see, to reassure myself she was okay. Those small pockets of normalcy mattered more than I realized at the time.

Eating while the food was still warm felt like a luxury. Privacy became something I vaguely remembered, like a version of life that belonged to someone else. My body no longer felt fully mine. It felt borrowed. Shared. Stretched thin by the constant pull of another person's needs.

If you are recovering from surgery, there is another layer of humility added to the mix. Every movement becomes deliberate. I learned how to brace myself before standing.

How to move slowly, carefully, as if my body might split open again if I rushed it. Sneezing became something I prepared for. Laughing was measured. Pain was no longer abstract. It was specific and sharp and instructive. It taught me where my limits were and how to respect them.

There is nothing glamorous about postpartum recovery. It is raw and practical and deeply unromantic. My baby and I both wore diapers. Mesh underwear became my uniform. Bathroom trips required planning and patience. My body leaked. Swelled. Bruised. Adjusted. And still, beneath the discomfort, there was awe. My body felt foreign and fragile, but it was also undeniable proof of resilience. It had carried life. It had endured trauma. It was healing in real time.

Emotionally, everything felt closer to the surface.

I cried easily. Sometimes from joy that caught me off guard. Sometimes from grief I couldn't quite name. Sometimes because the weight of responsibility pressed in all at once. Hormones surged and settled unpredictably, leaving me unsure whether what I was feeling was temporary or foundational. I could feel deeply connected to my baby and deeply disconnected from myself in the same breath. I missed parts of my old life even as I fell in love with this new one.

Both truths existed together.

Neither canceled the other out.

There was grief in that tension. Not because I regretted becoming a mother, but because I missed the ease of who I used to be. The woman who could leave the house without planning. Who could say yes impulsively. Who could rest without guilt. The spontaneous life I once had did not disappear overnight, but it slipped quietly out of reach, replaced by a schedule dictated by someone else's needs.

What I had not expected was the mourning that came with that realization. The understanding that no matter how deeply I wanted this, no matter how fiercely I loved being a mother, I would never not be someone's mother again. There was no off switch. No temporary return. Even in moments of joy, even when motherhood felt like the greatest alignment of my life, I sometimes mourned the identity, the freedoms, the hobbies, and the version of myself who existed without constant responsibility. Wanting this life did not erase the loss of the one that came before it.

Feeding became its own emotional landscape, one few people warn you about and almost everyone has an opinion on. From the beginning, the pressure was constant. In hospital rooms. In pediatrician offices. In late-night internet searches and well-meaning comments. Somehow, no matter the method, the responsibility always felt like it landed squarely on me. My body. My choices. My burden to get it right.

The exhaustion compounded everything. Feeding was relentless in its timing. Every few hours. Around the clock. There were no true breaks. I measured ounces. Tracked minutes. Watched my baby for cues and myself for signs of failure. Even moments meant to feel bonding carried tension when I worried about supply, latch, weight gain. The intimacy of feeding became layered with performance, and that stole joy from a moment already demanding everything I had.

Lyme disease entered my postpartum story quietly, complicating everything. Because I was breastfeeding, treatment options were limited. We tried what felt safest. Within a week, my baby developed a rash. One doctor said it was the medication. Another said it couldn't be. I stood between conflicting opinions, holding a rash-covered newborn and carrying the weight of a choice no one prepares you for.

Continue breastfeeding and risk her reaction, or stop and let my body heal.

I stopped breastfeeding. The rash disappeared almost immediately. Relief came quickly. Guilt followed close behind.

The guilt surprised me with its persistence. I knew my baby was fed. That she was growing. That she was safe. But motherhood is not lived in logic alone. I mourned the feeding story I had imagined. The closeness. The simplicity. The sense of doing it "right."

When I had to pump and dump during antibiotics, my supply plummeted. I tried everything to bring it back. Teas. Cookies. Supplements. Oatmeal. Electrolyte drinks. Weekly weight checks felt brutal. Each number carried more meaning than it should have.

By the fourth month, we switched fully to formula. Opinions followed. But my benchmark had shifted. She was fed. She was growing. She was content.

That was enough.

The loneliness of the fourth trimester settled in quietly. Maternity leave was a strange kind of isolation. I was never truly alone, yet profoundly cut off from the world I once belonged to. Friends returned to routines. Coworkers moved forward without me. The world kept spinning while my universe narrowed to feedings, naps, and the constant mental tally of what my baby might need next.

Her dad returned to work after only two weeks. Not because we were ready, but because we needed the income. I stood in the doorway that first morning, holding our baby, watching him leave, grateful and heartbroken all at once. He wanted to be there. He wanted the middle-of-the-night feeds, the quiet hours of bonding. Instead, he carried the weight of providing, often alone.

This is the part of postpartum life rarely spoken about honestly. The strain. The separation. The way love and responsibility pull partners in different directions. One staying home, physically present but exhausted. The other leaving each day, physically absent but emotionally tethered.

Returning to work at twelve weeks felt like being split in two. I stepped back into a world that had continued on without me, while mine had been entirely redefined. My clothes didn't fit the same. My emotions didn't sit the same. My heart ached in ways I had never known.

And yet, in the middle of the exhaustion, something steady grew. A quiet confidence. Not the loud kind. The kind that forms through repetition. Through getting up again. Through learning your baby's cues. Through realizing you are doing something profoundly difficult and surviving it.

The fourth trimester does not announce its end. One day, you simply realize you are standing again. Still tired. Still learning. But no longer underwater.

You are becoming.

For the Mama in It Right Now:

If you are in the thick of this season, exhausted in ways you didn't know were possible, please know this: nothing about the fourth trimester is supposed to feel easy or graceful. You are not failing because you feel overwhelmed. You are not weak because you need rest, help, reassurance, or a moment to breathe. Your body is healing from something immense. Your heart is learning a love that asks everything of you. You and your baby are strangers becoming each other's safest place, and that kind of learning is tender and messy and slow.

It is okay if you don't recognize yourself right now. It is okay if your emotions feel big, unpredictable, or heavy. It is okay if you grieve the version of early motherhood you imagined while still loving your baby fiercely. You are allowed to rest without guilt. You are allowed to make choices that protect both you and your child. You are allowed to release expectations that no longer serve you.

You are not meant to do this alone, and you are not meant to do it perfectly. Showing up, again and again, even when you feel unsure, even when your body aches, even when your heart feels stretched thin, is enough. You are becoming a mother in real time. And that becoming, exactly as it is, is worthy of gentleness, patience, and compassion.

What I Wish I Knew Then:

- The fourth trimester is tender and raw for everyone.
- You are not supposed to know how to do this yet. You are still learning from each other.
- Rest is allowed, and encouraged.
- Being overwhelmed does not mean you're doing something wrong.
- You are not alone, even when it feels like you are.

7

Learning to Love the Different Way

I did not expect to fall more in love with my boyfriend by watching him become a parent.

I thought I would feel grateful. Relieved. Appreciative in a practical way. I imagined partnership as something functional. Shared responsibility. Split shifts. Someone handing you water while you bounce a crying baby at three in the morning. I assumed love would show up in logistics. In fairness. In efficiency. In survival. I believed teamwork would feel necessary and helpful, like a system built to keep us afloat through the exhaustion.

What I did not expect was how much it would stretch me.

How quickly it would reach parts of me I had not examined yet. How it would challenge my sense of control, my identity as her mother, and the quiet belief I carried that loving her best meant doing things my way. I did not expect to learn so early that trust is not theoretical. It is lived. It is practiced in ordinary moments, when you have to decide whether to hold tighter or step back.

The love that grew between us was not dramatic.

There were no sweeping gestures or perfectly timed words. It was quieter than that. Steadier. It lived in moments so ordinary they were easy to miss. Moments that do not photograph well or translate into stories, yet somehow carry the most weight. It lived in repetition. In showing up again and again, especially when tired.

It showed up in the way he reached for her the moment she fussed, even if he had just walked in after a long day. It showed up in how his voice softened without effort, as if gentleness came naturally rather than through instruction. It showed up in the way he stayed with her when she cried. He did not rush to fix it. He did not hand her back to me at the first sign of uncertainty. He stayed long enough to learn her. Watching him figure it out reminded me that parenting is not something you master. It is something you enter into, imperfectly and sincerely.

Alongside that admiration, something else stirred.

Watching him parent our daughter was beautiful.

And if I am honest, it was also deeply uncomfortable.

Not because he was doing anything wrong.

But because he was doing things differently.

That difference unsettled me more than I expected. I felt it as a tightening in my chest. An urge to step in, to correct or redirect. To explain how I did things and why my way worked. The feeling came quickly and quietly, often disguised as helpfulness or concern. I told myself it was about consistency. About what was best for her. About preventing confusion.

Underneath all of that was something harder to admit.

Fear.

Fear of losing my footing in a role that had quickly become central to who I was. Fear that if someone else could soothe her, read her cues, and meet her needs, then maybe I was not as essential as I needed to believe. Fear that the routines I had built, the ones that grounded me when everything else felt unsteady, could exist without me at the center.

Those routines were not just habits.

They were proof.

Proof that I knew her.

Proof that I was capable.

Proof that I was doing this right.

Watching someone else step into that space forced a quiet reckoning. Not jealousy. Not resentment. Just the realization that motherhood, as much as it roots you, also asks you to loosen your grip. Love does not disappear when it is shared, but learning that can feel like loss before it feels like relief.

For many mothers, this moment arrives in different ways.

It might be a partner. A grandparent. A caregiver. Or simply time, as your child grows and reaches for independence. It may come the first time someone else feeds your baby, soothes a tantrum, or becomes the preferred comfort. It is the moment you realize that loving well does not always require control. That connection does not vanish because someone else can meet your child where they are. Sharing that space can feel freeing and frightening at the same time.

The truth was that we were both exhausted, just in very different ways.

My exhaustion came from constancy. From being needed without pause. From carrying the invisible map of her world everywhere I went. When she last ate. How long she slept. What this cry meant compared to the last one. My tiredness followed me even into sleep. It was vigilance wrapped in love, responsibility that never fully powered down.

His exhaustion came from outward pressure. Long hours. Work demands. The weight of providing. He came home depleted but eager. He wanted to help. He wanted to bond. He wanted to step into a rhythm that had been established without him. Parenting did not pause while he was away, and finding his place inside it required patience from both of us.

Two people, both tired.

Two roles, both heavy.

One shared love, trying to find room to breathe.

What softened me was not a single conversation or dramatic breakthrough.

It happened quietly, over time. Through observation. Through restraint. Through choosing, again and again, to pause instead of intervene. To watch instead of correct. To let discomfort rise without immediately trying to manage it away.

The first time I left the house alone for more than a quick errand felt bigger than it should have. A haircut. A nail appointment. Ordinary things I once did without thinking. I remember sitting in the chair, cape around my shoulders, hands resting in my lap, aware of how unfamiliar it felt to be away. My phone sat beside me, screen dark but heavy. I wanted to text him. Not because I did not trust him. Not because I thought something would go wrong. But because checking in had become second nature. Because staying connected had started to feel like staying in control.

I reminded myself, gently but firmly, to let the moment be. I resisted asking how things were going, not because I did not care, but because I did. I wanted him to feel trusted, not watched. I wanted him to move through those hours with her without my presence hovering nearby.

So I stayed quiet.

I let the time pass.

In that small act of restraint, something shifted.

Trust, I was learning, is not just believing someone can do it. It is giving them the space to do it without supervision.

In that space, I saw what I could no longer deny.

He was learning her in ways that could not be taught. Not through schedules taped to the fridge or apps or mental checklists built through repetition, but through presence. He learned her by staying. By watching. By listening. He learned the weight of her in his arms. The subtle changes in her cries. The way her breathing softened when she finally relaxed. I watched her body melt against him, tension leaving her limbs as if she knew, without question, that she was safe there.

She responded to his voice before she saw his face. A pause would come over her, a small stillness that felt intentional. Trust lived there. Quiet and unmistakable. Their bond unfolded on its own timeline, shaped by his presence and her openness, not by comparison to mine.

It did not mirror my relationship with her.

And it did not need to.

She did not need him to parent like me to feel safe.

That realization shifted something fundamental inside me. It challenged my belief that safety comes from sameness. From uniform routines. From doing things one right way. It asked me to trust that love is not diminished by difference. It grows through it.

With that understanding came two emotions, living side by side.

Relief, in knowing I did not have to carry everything alone. That I was not the sole keeper of her comfort or security. That someone else could hold her with the same care, allowing me moments to rest, to exhale, to step back without fear.

And grief, in recognizing how tightly I had been holding on. How much of my identity had wrapped itself around being the one who knew best, the one who could soothe her fastest, the one whose presence felt most essential. Letting go, even slightly, felt like releasing something fragile I had built carefully in those early, uncertain days.

Letting go did not diminish my role.

It expanded it.

It made room for something stronger than control.

Trust.

Trust in him.

Trust in her.

Trust that love does not need to be guarded so fiercely to remain intact.

Parenting, I learned, is not a synchronized performance.

It is not two people moving in perfect rhythm, never missing a cue. It is a commitment made in real time. One shaped by exhaustion, uncertainty, and constant adjustment. It is learning to pass the weight back and forth without keeping score. It is accepting that balance is not fixed. It shifts. It wavers. It returns.

Some days we move easily, communicating without effort. Some days one of us carries more while the other regroups. Some days I am steady. Some days he is. And on the hardest days, when neither of us feels steady at all, we still show up. We still choose each other. We still choose her.

That choice matters more than perfection ever could.

Family does not take shape through flawless routines or identical approaches. It forms through commitment. Through staying, even when things feel messy and unfinished.

There were moments of friction. Exhaustion sharpened words that would otherwise be gentle. Stress magnified small miscommunications. Parenting has a way of revealing every crack. Beneath it all, something steady remained. We were not opponents. We were on the same side, facing the same unknowns, learning as we went.

Watching him parent taught me that love lives in persistence.

In showing up when you are unsure.

In staying present when things feel unfamiliar.

In trying again without needing to be perfect.

It taught me that partnership is not about doing things the same way. It is about trusting the other person's heart. Trusting that their intentions are rooted in care, even when their approach looks different from yours.

The more I let go, the more space opened.

Space for admiration.

Space for gratitude.

Space for love to deepen instead of tightening around fear.

I was not just falling in love with the father he was becoming. I was falling in love with the way he learned without defensiveness. With the way he carried responsibility without being asked. With the way he showed our daughter, again and again, that she was safe in his arms too.

Parenting reshaped my understanding of motherhood.

It reshaped my understanding of partnership.

It taught me that building a family is not about perfection. It is about shared intention. Mutual effort. The quiet, ordinary decision to keep showing up together.

And somewhere between difference and devotion, something beautiful took root.

Not just a family.

But a deeper love than I ever expected to find.

For the Mama in it Right Now:

If you are struggling to release control, if watching your partner do things differently makes your chest tighten, know this: your way is not the only way. It is simply the way you know best right now. It is the way you learned through trial and error, through long days and longer nights, through instinct and exhaustion and love. Of course it feels personal. Of course it feels fragile. You worked hard to learn your baby, and letting someone else step into that space can feel like losing your footing.

If you find yourself correcting, hovering, or feeling irritated by things that don't truly matter, pause and breathe. That reaction is not about distrust. It is about fear. Fear of getting it wrong. Fear of losing connection. Fear of carrying the weight alone and needing things to stay predictable just to survive the day. None of that makes you a bad partner or a controlling parent. It makes you human in a season that asks too much of you.

His way will become its own kind of magic. It may not look like yours. It may feel slower, messier, or unfamiliar. But it will grow into something steady and meaningful for your child, just as your way already has. Your baby does not need one perfect method. They need two people who love them, show up for them, and are willing to learn.

Two exhausted parents can love each other deeply while also feeling overwhelmed, irritated, disconnected, or unsure. Both things can be true. You are allowed to need help and still struggle to accept it. You are allowed to feel gratitude and tension at the same time. Early parenting stretches relationships not because they are weak, but because they are being asked to grow in new directions all at once.

You are a team, even on the days it feels fragile or strained. Even on the days you speak sharply or retreat inward. Even on the days you both feel like you are giving everything you have and still coming up short. Teamwork in this season does not look like perfection. It looks like repair. It looks like learning. It looks like choosing each other again, even when you are tired beyond words.

You do not have to carry this alone. And you do not have to control everything to keep your child safe and loved. Sometimes the bravest thing you can do is loosen your grip and trust that love can take more than one form.

You are doing better than you think.

What I Wish I Knew Then:

- Different doesn't mean wrong. It only means different.
- Your child won't remember how perfectly you swaddled, but they will remember how safe they felt with both of you
- The stress of this season will not last forever. This is your family learning how to function together, imperfectly and wholeheartedly.

8

Now I Understand

Motherhood has a way of rearranging time.

It does not only change the present or redraw the future. It reaches backward, quietly and persistently, and reorders the past. It shines a different light on memories you thought you understood, sacrifices you once overlooked, and questions you never thought to ask. It softens your gaze. It sharpens your empathy. It teaches you to see your own mother not just as she was, but as who she had to be. And in doing so, it offers an unexpected gift: the chance to carry that understanding forward with intention.

Before I became a mother, I thought I understood my mom's exhaustion.

I noticed how tired she looked at the end of long days. I saw how she moved through the house on autopilot, how she powered through responsibilities even when her body clearly wanted rest. I recognized her fatigue in a general, surface-level way. But I did not understand it until I felt my own bone-deep exhaustion. The kind that settles into your muscles and thoughts and never fully leaves. The kind that comes from being needed constantly, from knowing there is no pause button, no off switch, no moment where the responsibility truly stops.

Only then did I begin to understand how much endurance that kind of love requires and how quietly powerful it is.

Only then did I begin to understand how often she must have put herself last so my brother and I could come first.

How many times she swallowed her own needs so mine could be met. How often she carried fear quietly so I could feel safe. How much emotional labor she shouldered without acknowledgment, the invisible work of keeping a household running and a family steady.

There are years I wish I could soften in hindsight. Years as a teenager when I was convinced that independence required opposition, that my parents' concern was ignorance rather than love. I regret the strain I placed on our relationship before I had the capacity to understand how much patience my mom was practicing in those moments.

I did not understand what it took to love us through every phase, through tantrums and defiance, through slammed doors and stubborn silences, through stages that demanded something new from her each time.

Motherhood placed that same responsibility into my own hands and whispered, *now you know.*

And with that knowing came not just humility, but a deeper respect for the quiet competence I had once taken for granted.

And just as I was beginning to find my footing in early motherhood, another weight settled onto my shoulders, one I could never have prepared for.

Shortly after my daughter was born, my mother was diagnosed with Stage 4 Mantle Cell Lymphoma.

The words felt unreal, like they belonged to someone else's life. My mother, the steady one, the strong one, the person who had always shown up without hesitation, suddenly became fragile in a way I had never known her to be. The shift was disorienting. It felt like the ground beneath us had changed shape without warning. And yet, even in that uncertainty, her presence remained steady, a reminder that strength does not disappear when vulnerability arrives.

What made it even harder was knowing how much she had carried me through pregnancy and birth.

She had been my anchor long before her diagnosis. The steady voice on the other end of nervous phone calls. The reassuring presence at appointments when my boyfriend's work kept him away. During labor, she never left the hospital. She stayed through every hour, every update, every moment of uncertainty. Not because she had to, but because she chose to. She was there not only for the arrival of her granddaughter, but for me.

Her devotion was quiet and unwavering.

It did not ask for praise or recognition. It simply existed. And in witnessing it as an adult, I began to understand how love matures, not louder, but deeper.

In the months that followed, she became my anchor in ways I did not even know I needed.

When my boyfriend had to work out of town, she stayed overnight so I would not feel the crushing isolation that can creep into early motherhood. She was my first call for everything. The small worries. The big fears. The moments when I felt unsure, overwhelmed, or convinced I was failing.

She showed up every single time.

And in her constancy, she modeled something I did not yet

know I was learning: how to be present without trying to fix, how to love without requiring certainty.

And she did so while navigating her own fear, her own exhaustion, her own uncertainty about what the future might hold.

She was facing a life-altering diagnosis, endless appointments, and an unclear treatment path. And yet she made sure I never felt alone. She did not burden me with her fear. She did not pull away. Instead, she leaned in. She loved me through one of the most vulnerable seasons of my life while quietly enduring one of the hardest seasons of her own.

Her presence became both a comfort and a compass. A reminder of what matters when everything else feels fragile.

Becoming a mother cracked open a deeper understanding of who she was.

Not just the version of her I knew growing up, but the woman behind it. The one who stayed awake worrying long after I insisted I was fine. The one who prayed silently, protected fiercely, and believed relentlessly. The one who fought battles I never saw and carried burdens she never discussed.

And in seeing her more clearly, I felt a quiet responsibility emerge. Not to replicate her exactly, but to honor what she taught me through care.

When I was younger, I thought she worried too much. I thought she didn't trust me enough. I thought she overreacted. Now I know she understood far more than I ever did.

She saw danger where I saw freedom. She saw risk where I saw opportunity. She held the full picture of me long before I had the capacity to see myself clearly. And now I understand how heavy that kind of love is. How constant. How consuming. How brave.

Understanding this did not make me feel trapped by love. It made me feel steadied by it.

I hear her voice come out of my own mouth in moments I never expected.

I catch myself repeating her phrases, her warnings, her gentleness. I feel her instincts rise up in me when my daughter cries, stumbles, or reaches for reassurance. I understand now how her heart must have clenched as she watched me grow. How pride and fear must have coexisted in every milestone. How letting go never meant loving less.

Motherhood humbled me into realizing that the version of my mother I saw as a child was only a fraction of who she truly was.

I did not understand how much she gave up. How much she carried quietly. How much she held together without recognition. Only now, while juggling my own endless list, forgetting half of it, and feeling guilty about the rest, do I see how seamlessly she did it all. And seeing that does not diminish me. It strengthens me.

There have been countless moments since my daughter was born when I have whispered to myself, *this is what she felt.*

The fear when a fever spikes in the middle of the night. The worry when it is too quiet. The ache of leaving, even briefly. The guilt of wanting time alone. The heartbreak of watching your child cry when you cannot fix it.

And in recognizing those moments, I've found compassion. For her, and for myself.

Motherhood did not give me this understanding all at once.

It arrived in fragments. In sleepless nights and messy days. In moments of doubt and flashes of joy. In tiny victories that felt enormous. In the way my daughter's laugh could undo an entire day's worth of stress in an instant. And with each fragment, my gratitude deepened, not out of obligation, but out of clarity.

And once I felt that love fully, undeniably, I understood the depth of love my mother must have felt for me.

A love that is fierce and fragile at the same time. A love that wants to shelter and strengthen, protect and prepare. A love that is exhausting and exquisite, ordinary and sacred all at once.

I used to think my mom held on too tightly.

Now I know there is no such thing as too tightly. There is only a mother trying every single day with everything she has. Choosing steadiness over ease. Choosing presence over perfection. Choosing love even when it costs her comfort, her rest, and her sense of self.

When I look back now, I do not see things the way I once did.

I see presence. Steady. Imperfect. Dependable presence. And in seeing that, I feel hope, not pressure, for the kind of mother I am becoming.

Motherhood did not just change how I see myself.

It changed how I see my own mother.

It gave me the opportunity to love her more fully, more generously, and more honestly than I ever could before. And now, as I raise my own child, I feel her everywhere. In my instincts. In my softness. In my resolve. In the parts of me that choose love even when it is inconvenient or exhausting or uncomfortable.

I understand her now. Not just as my mother, but as a woman navigating responsibility, fear, hope, and love all at once. And I love her not only for the mother she was and is, but for the woman she had to become to be her.

Motherhood is relentless. It is messy. It asks more of you

than you think you have.

And because of that, it sharpens your vision. It opens your eyes. It creates gratitude that feels sacred, not because it is owed, but because it is earned through understanding.

Now I know.

Now I understand.

Now I see her.

And in seeing her more clearly, I feel more capable of becoming the kind of mother my daughter will one day understand too.

Mom, I am so deeply, profoundly grateful.

For the Mama in It Right Now:

If motherhood has started to change the way you see your own mother, you are not imagining it. That shift, that sudden tenderness, that ache that arrives without warning, it is part of the transformation. You are standing in a place where past and present collide, where memory meets understanding, where love deepens in ways that feel almost overwhelming. It makes sense if you feel flooded with gratitude one moment and grief the next. It makes sense if you wish you could go back and soften moments that once felt sharp, or if you find yourself missing her even when she is right there.

If your relationship with your mother is loving but complicated, close but evolving, distant but still emotionally loud, you are not doing motherhood wrong. Becoming a mother does not rewrite your history, but it does give it new context. You may see sacrifices you never noticed, wounds you never understood, or strengths you never fully appreciated. You may also notice places where things still hurt. All of that is allowed. Growth does not require a clean or perfect relationship. It requires honesty, curiosity, and compassion, especially toward yourself.

If your mother is still your safe place, your first call, your steady ground, let yourself lean into that without guilt. Needing your mom does not make you less capable or less strong. It makes you human. And if you are mothering while also watching your own mother navigate illness, aging, or vulnerability, it is okay if that feels heavy in ways you cannot fully name. Loving both up and down generations at once is tender work. It stretches the heart in directions no one prepares you for.

And if your relationship with your mother is strained, fractured, or painful, this chapter may stir things you were not expecting. Becoming a mother can open questions you never planned to ask. It can surface grief for what you needed and did not receive, alongside determination to do things differently. That awareness is not betrayal. It is clarity. You are allowed to honor what was good, mourn what was missing, and still move forward with intention.

Wherever you find yourself, know this: the tenderness you feel is not weakness. It is evidence of growth. The way motherhood cracks you open and invites deeper understanding is not accidental. You are learning a new language, one spoken in instinct, empathy, and love. You are allowed to feel all of it. You are allowed to take your time. And you are allowed to become someone new while still holding space for who you have been.

You are not alone in this reckoning. You are becoming, and that is sacred work.

What I Wish I Knew Then

- That gratitude can arrive years later and still matter.

- That becoming a mom would unlock a new language; one only she and I now speak.
- That the love she carries for me is bigger, deeper, and more relentless than I could have imagined.

9

Redefining Me

Motherhood required me to redefine myself in ways I did not see coming. Not all at once. Not dramatically. But steadily, persistently, until I could no longer pretend I was the same person I had been before. And while that realization felt destabilizing at first, it also carried an invitation. To pause. To reassess. To choose more deliberately who I wanted to be moving forward.

I was no longer just a partner, a daughter, a friend, or a professional moving through the world with familiar markers of identity. I was someone's mom. That single word carried a gravity I had not fully anticipated. It rearranged the hierarchy of my life and quietly asked questions I had never been forced to answer before. *Who am I when I am not producing, achieving, helping, or proving something? Who am I when my worth is no longer measured by output, but by presence? Who am I when the world expects me to fold every other part of myself into this one role and call it fulfillment?*

And underneath those questions, there was space. Space to define the answers for myself.

Becoming a mother did not erase the woman I was before, but she no longer fit the same way. I felt like an old favorite sweater pulled from the back of a drawer. Familiar. Comforting. And suddenly tight in places that once felt easy. I kept tugging at the seams, trying to stretch her back into shape, until I realized the work was not in forcing a return. It was in allowing room for something new to take form.

There was grief in that tension.

Not because there was any part of me that regretted becoming a mother, but because I missed the ease of who I used to be. The woman who could leave the house without planning. Who could say yes impulsively. Who could rest without guilt. The spontaneous life I once had did not disappear overnight, but it slipped quietly out of reach, replaced by a schedule dictated by someone else's needs. And still, within that structure, I began to notice a different kind of freedom taking root. One built on intention rather than impulse.

What I had not expected was the period of mourning that came with that realization. The understanding that no matter how deeply I wanted this, no matter how fiercely I loved being a mother, I would never not be someone's mother again. There was no off switch, no temporary return to who I was before. Even in moments of joy, even when motherhood felt like the greatest alignment of my life, I sometimes mourned the identity, the freedoms, the hobbies, and the version of myself who existed without constant responsibility. And yet, alongside that loss, there was meaning. A sense of permanence that felt grounding rather than limiting. This role was not something I could step away from, but it was something I could grow into.

And while people encouraged me to embrace this new identity, to be grateful, to lean into it fully, there were moments when that encouragement felt dismissive. As if missing parts of myself meant I was doing motherhood wrong. As if love should cancel out longing. But I'm here to tell you that grief and gratitude can coexist. Becoming a mother did not mean I stopped being me. It meant I was learning how to hold who I was, who I am, and who I am still becoming, all at once.

Motherhood is a study in contradiction.

Exhaustion exists beside awe.

Overwhelm sits shoulder to shoulder with joy.

Independence collides with surrender.

And in learning to hold opposites, I was learning a new kind of strength. One rooted not in certainty, but in flexibility.

I was learning to love this life fiercely while still grieving pieces of the one I had known. To feel grateful and depleted in the same breath. To feel anchored and untethered all at once. The duality was dizzying, but it was also expansive. It widened my emotional range. It taught me that complexity was not a flaw, but a feature of growth.

I loved being with my daughter, and I missed myself. I cherished the closeness, the way her body fit so naturally against mine, the way my arms felt like home to her. And I craved space so intensely it made my chest ache. Every milestone felt magical and mildly terrifying at the same time. And slowly, I learned that this did not make me ungrateful. It made me human.

I felt the quiet tension between who I had been in the world and who I was now expected to be. Before motherhood, I had spent years building a career, cultivating ambition, and finding meaning in work that asked something of me. I was used to long hours, full calendars, and the quiet pressure to always be available. I struggled to say no. Work often came first, not because it had to, but because I had trained myself to believe that productivity equaled worth. After my daughter arrived, my priorities shifted in ways I could not ignore. Home life began to matter more than work in a way that felt both unsettling and clarifying. I started holding boundaries I had never practiced before. Saying no became less about guilt and more about protection. Not of my time, but of my family, my energy, and the life I was building at home.

That internal conflict was exhausting. Loving my child deeply while still wanting to honor the parts of myself that existed long before her. Wanting to be fully present at home while also craving engagement with the world beyond it. There were days when I felt split in two, unsure which version of myself deserved more attention. Over time, I learned something important. Redefining myself did not have to mean reducing myself. It could mean refining. Reordering. Choosing with intention rather than guilt.

Friendships shifted in ways I had not expected.

Some deepened, strengthened by the honesty that only survival mode allows. I became deeply grateful for the friends who understood when responses to texts took hours or sometimes days. The ones who did not interpret silence as distance. The ones who still tried to make plans instead of assuming I could not. Being asked mattered more than they probably realized. It reminded me that I still belonged. That I was still wanted.

I was especially grateful for the friends who came to me. Who were content sitting in a living room, catching up between feedings and naps. The ones who welcomed my child into their arms with such love, care, and adoration, while also always seeing me too. They did not treat motherhood as something that erased me. They held space for both. In their presence, I felt whole.

Others faded quietly.

Not because of conflict or resentment, but because our lives no longer moved at the same pace. They lived in a world shaped by spontaneity and flexibility. I lived in a world measured in nap windows, feedings, and how much energy I had left at the end of the day. The distance hurt, but it also clarified something. Not every relationship is meant to come forward unchanged. Some belong to a previous season, and letting them rest makes room for connections that fit who you are becoming.

Even when I did see people, I worried about becoming boring. About being reduced to a single note. About conversations circling endlessly around sleep schedules and developmental milestones. But over time, I realized that depth does not disappear when life narrows. It concentrates. My world may have grown smaller, but it also grew more intentional. The things that remained mattered more.

The loneliness still surprised me.

I was rarely alone. Always needed. Always touched. And still, there was an ache to be seen as more than a role. To be recognized beyond what I provided. Motherhood can be isolating not because you lack company, but because you are becoming someone new in a world that does not always pause long enough to witness the shift. And yet, in that quiet, something unexpected happened. With fewer external markers to cling to, I began to notice myself more clearly. Not who I was expected to be, but who I was choosing to become.

Even my closet became a site of redefinition.

I stood staring at clothes I once loved, holding them up and wondering whether a mother should wear them. The question lingered longer than it should have. Over time, it softened.

What felt like me now. What supported the life I was living. What allowed me to move comfortably through days shaped by care and unpredictability. Choosing became less about holding on to who I had been and more about trusting who I was becoming.

The mom haircut arrived as a practical decision, but it carried more meaning than I expected. I cut my hair not because I wanted a new look, but because long hair required time and care I no longer had. It tangled in small hands. It asked for attention I was already giving elsewhere. As the strands fell, I did not just feel loss. I felt relief. Lightness. A quiet recognition that adaptation could be its own form of empowerment.

Guilt followed nearly everything.

Guilt for missing freedom.

Guilt for needing space.

Guilt for wanting quiet.

Guilt for longing to feel like myself again.

But beneath it, something else began to grow.

Motherhood stripped away performance.

It asked me who I was without constant validation. Without productivity as proof of worth. Without the need to explain or justify my choices. Slowly, I began to answer. I accepted help without apology. I said no and meant it. I chose sustainability over martyrdom. I allowed myself to become someone I respected, not just someone who endured.

Redefining myself did not happen all at once.

It happened through small permissions. Through moments of courage that looked ordinary from the outside. Through letting go of who I thought I had to be and allowing myself to become someone more honest, more grounded, more whole.

Motherhood, I learned, is not about losing yourself.

It is about expansion.

It is ongoing.

It is disorienting.

It is beautiful.

Grief and joy do not cancel each other out. They sharpen each other. They deepen your capacity. They make room for a fuller, truer version of who you are becoming.

And maybe that is the truest work of this season.

Holding who you were.

Honoring who you are becoming.

Offering grace to every version of yourself in between.

Not shrinking.

Not disappearing.

But growing quietly and profoundly into someone new.

For the Mama in It Right Now

If you are loving your baby fiercely while quietly missing pieces of yourself, nothing is wrong with you. That ache does not mean you regret motherhood. It means you are human. You are allowed to grieve versions of yourself even as you embrace the one forming now. You do not have to choose between gratitude and longing. They can live in the same breath.

If friendships feel harder, if your world feels smaller, if your identity feels unfamiliar, know that this is not loss, it is transition. You are in the middle of becoming. The redefining is not a failure. It is evidence that you are growing.

You are not selfish for needing space, rest, or quiet. You are not failing because your capacity looks different now. You are learning how to carry love for your child and yourself at the same time, and that takes practice.

You do not have to rush this process. You are allowed to move slowly. You are allowed to be unfinished. You are allowed to exist as a woman and a mother without having it all figured out yet.

What I Wish I Knew Then

- Motherhood is not a clean before and after. It is continuous evolution.
- Contradictions are not weakness. They are growth.
- Your worth is not measured by output but by presence.
- Some relationships will change, and that does not mean you failed.
- Guilt is not a verdict. It is a signal of care.
- Finding yourself again is not a return. It is a rebirth.

10

Presence Over Performance

No one warned me that perfection would arrive disguised as responsibility. That it would sound like love. Like effort. Like devotion. That it would feel noble and necessary, even righteous. That the pressure to do everything "right" would not burst into my life dramatically, but would slip in quietly, almost convincingly, whispering that if I just tried harder, planned better, stayed more organized, I would finally feel like I was doing motherhood correctly.

In the first year of parenting, it is nearly impossible not to believe this. You are already unsure. Already tired. Already carrying the weight of knowing that someone depends on you for everything. The stakes feel enormous. The margin for error feels impossibly small. I remember standing in the kitchen late at night, scrolling through articles with one hand while rocking my daughter with the other, convinced that somewhere online was the answer I was missing. If I could just read one more thing, track one more detail, I would finally feel settled.

And so responsibility quietly morphed into performance. Care turned into comparison. Love started asking for proof.

It did not help that everywhere I looked, motherhood appeared polished. My phone filled with smiling babies, serene parents, spotless homes, color-coordinated routines. Even the struggles were softened. Curated. Framed as growth. Without realizing it, I began measuring my insides against other people's outsides. I assumed everyone else knew something I did not. That they had found a rhythm I was failing to grasp.

And so I tried harder.

I tried to optimize sleep.

I tracked feedings.

I analyzed wake windows.

I worried about development and stimulation and whether I was doing too much or not enough.

I second-guessed instincts that had served me well only days before.

Motherhood began to feel like something I could get wrong if I was not careful enough.

Perfection did not settle me. It tightened me.

It seeped into the smallest corners of my life. It showed up in milestone photos that suddenly felt like they required perfect lighting, the right outfit, the right timing. I remember changing my daughter's clothes twice before a picture, frustrated when she fussed instead of smiling, as if the moment itself was failing to cooperate. It showed up in birthday parties planned for babies who would not remember any of it, but somehow felt like a reflection of my competence. It showed up in comparing my child's progress to charts and strangers and timelines that did not know her at all.

Beneath all of it lived an unspoken fear.

If I do not get this right, it means something about me.

About my love.

About my worth.

What no one tells you is how easily those "perfect" moments begin to overshadow the real ones. I started documenting more than living. Thinking ahead instead of staying present. Planning joy instead of noticing it when it arrived. I worried about whether things looked right instead of whether they felt right. The highlight reel began stealing the highlight.

And still, the truth remained stubbornly simple.

My baby did not need me to perform.

She needed me to be present.

She did not care about curated spaces or carefully executed plans. She cared about safety. About familiarity. About being seen and responded to. She cared about the arms that reached for her when she cried. The voice that met her when she babbled. The face she searched for when the world felt overwhelming.

Children are shaped by connection, not perfection. They are shaped by responsiveness. By repair. By the way you come back after hard moments. Long before they remember anything you tried to make look right, they remember how it felt to be with you.

This lesson landed for me when I planned my daughter's first birthday.

I treated it like a production. I chose a theme. Coordinated decorations. Booked a venue. Planned a menu she could barely eat. I spent time and energy on details that felt wildly disproportionate to the moment itself. Somewhere along the way, I convinced myself that doing it well meant doing it impressively. That the success of the day reflected something essential about me as her mother.

The pressure sat heavy in my chest.

And then the day came.

Like so many moments in motherhood, it moved faster than I was ready for. The decorations blurred into the background. The cake was messy and crooked and deeply loved. Frosting ended up everywhere. The photos were chaotic and imperfect and full of motion. My daughter did not care about the details. She cared about familiar faces. About frosting on her hands. About the arms she could toddler toward when she needed grounding.

Standing there, watching her delight in something I had nearly overthought into misery, something softened in me.

Childhood does not need perfection.

It needs presence.

It needs laughter.

It needs connection.

That realization did not make me careless. It made me freer.

Because presence is not passive. It is active. It is choosing to put the phone down even when it buzzes. Choosing to sit on the floor instead of cleaning it right away. Choosing to meet your child where they are instead of where you think they should be. It is allowing moments to be enough without elevating them into something impressive or shareable.

I am learning to live in that space now. The imperfect. The unfinished. The deeply human. Motherhood happens in messy rooms and mismatched outfits. In days that unravel and still matter. In moments where nothing goes according to plan and everything essential still happens.

This is true whether you are parenting alone or with a partner. Whether you are working outside the home or staying home. Whether your baby sleeps through the night or never does. Whether you have support or are figuring it out as you go. The pressure to perform does not discriminate. It finds all of us eventually.

But presence is always available.

It is available when you sit beside your child instead of fixing the mess immediately.

When you listen instead of rushing.

When you choose connection over control.

And in those moments, stripped of expectation and performance, motherhood becomes unmistakably clear.

It was never about doing it perfectly.

It was always about being there.

For the Mama in It Right Now

If you are feeling the pressure to do everything right, to make every moment meaningful, to live up to a standard that always seems just out of reach, pause here. Breathe. Your baby does not need perfection from you. They need your warmth. Your voice. Your steadiness, even when you feel unsure.

It is okay if the photos are not perfect. It is okay if the party was simple. It is okay if today did not look the way you imagined it would. None of those things reflect your worth as a mother. Your child is not measuring your effort in details. They are feeling your presence.

You are not behind. You are not failing. You are not missing something everyone else has figured out. You are doing sacred work in real time, and that work is messy by nature. Let the pressure soften. Let the real moments matter more. You are already enough, even when you are exhausted, even when you feel uncertain, even when the day feels unfinished.

What I Wish I Knew Then:

- No one was living the perfect life I was comparing mine to.
- My baby was not keeping score of my worries.
- The first birthday was more for me than for her.
- Good enough parenting is not settling. It is grounded, healthy, and deeply loving.
- One day I would laugh at how much energy I spent on things that never mattered.
- Presence was always the point.

11

The Moments That Matter

Somewhere in the middle of the chaos, I learned that motherhood is not measured in milestones the way we are taught to believe.

Before having my daughter, I thought the big moments would define everything. The first steps. The first words. The clearly marked achievements that come with applause and photos and congratulatory texts. Those moments are sweet, of course. They matter. They deserve to be celebrated. But they are not what stays with you the longest. They do not hold the deepest weight.

What lingers are the moments you barely recognize while they are happening.

The ordinary ones.

The unremarkable ones.

The ones that pass quietly, without witnesses or documentation, and somehow rearrange your heart without asking for permission.

Our walks to daycare became one of those places. What I once treated as a transition, a task between destinations, slowed under her watchful eye. She stopped to smell flowers like they were something rare and essential. She crouched to examine rocks scattered along the sidewalk, lifting each one carefully, turning it over in her small hands as if it were a precious gem she had just discovered. I learned quickly that there was no such thing as "just a rock" anymore. Each one carried possibility. Texture. Story. Wonder.

Every airplane in the sky stopped us completely. She would point upward with urgency and awe, eyes wide, voice full of excitement, as if she were seeing the most incredible thing she had ever witnessed. Even if it was the fifth airplane that morning. Even if we had already stopped multiple times. Each one mattered. Each one was new. Her awareness was remarkable. Her presence absolute.

Loud noises became invitations instead of interruptions. Trucks rumbling past. Trains in the distance. Semis roaring by. Sounds I had long tuned out now sparked her curiosity, pulling us into shared moments of listening and watching. She stood still, absorbing it all, asking without words to stay just a little longer. Through her, I began to notice how much of the world I had been moving past without truly seeing.

There were nights when she melted into my chest during bedtime stories, her small weight anchoring me fully in the present. I would start reading with intention, determined to get through the book, to keep the routine moving, to stay on schedule. But inevitably, her body would soften, her breathing slowing as sleep crept in gently. Her head would settle against me with complete trust, and something in me would follow. The noise of the day faded. The unfinished tasks. The constant mental lists that never seemed to quiet. All of it softened as she slept, safe and warm and certain that I would stay.

Those moments asked nothing of me except stillness.

They reminded me that being needed does not always require action. Sometimes it requires restraint. Sometimes it requires choosing not to move, not to shift, not to rush, even when your arm is numb and your back aches and the clock says you should be doing something else.

There were car rides where I sang the same nursery songs on repeat. I sang because she watched me in the mirror like I was something magical. Like I was enough. Like my voice, tired and imperfect, was exactly what she needed. I sang even when my throat hurt, even when my patience felt thin, because her joy was immediate and unfiltered. She did not care about pitch or performance. She cared that I was there. That I was trying. That I was with her.

In those moments, I saw myself through her eyes.

Not as someone falling short.

Not as someone behind.

But as someone capable. Steady. Safe.

There were pauses too.

Moments when she crouched to study a bug as if it held the secrets of the universe. When she traced cracks in the sidewalk with her finger, following them slowly, deliberately, like a map only she could read. When she stopped mid-step to point out a shadow on the wall or another airplane overhead, fully absorbed by something I would have walked past without noticing.

She reminded me how to see again.

How to slow down without guilt.

How to let beauty exist without needing to explain or capture it.

Sticky fingers became proof of joy.

Giggles marked the passing of time.

Spontaneous hugs arrived without warning, often in the middle of mess or meltdown, wrapping around my legs when I least expected them.

Motherhood was never tidy. It unfolded between spills and tears, laughter and exhaustion. It lived in moments of patience stretched thin and then somehow replenished. It asked me to show up even when I felt depleted. And yet, the love woven through it all was steady. Expansive. Unconditional.

I stopped chasing perfection without even realizing I was doing it.

The shift was quiet. Gradual. Almost imperceptible.

The dishes could wait.

The laundry could pile up.

The to-do list could remain unfinished.

Presence mattered more than productivity. Sitting on the floor while she handed me the same toy again and again mattered more than accomplishing anything else. Listening to her narrate her world in fragments and repetition mattered more than efficiency. In those moments, nothing else felt as important as being exactly where she was, fully, without distraction.

Motherhood slowed me.

Sometimes gently.

Sometimes unwillingly.

It slowed me when she insisted on doing things herself, even when it would have been faster to step in. When she lingered over simple tasks, exploring them from every angle, unconcerned with deadlines or expectations. At first, the slowing felt frustrating. I was used to momentum. To progress. To moving forward.

But in that slowing, I began to notice everything.

The way her hand reached for mine when she felt unsure.

The way she offered me a rock like it was treasure, proud and earnest.

The way she looked back to make sure I was still there before moving forward, needing reassurance without words.

These moments rewrote me quietly and completely.

They taught me that safety is not something you announce. It is something you demonstrate, again and again, through small choices to stay close, to remain available, to let someone move at their own pace without rushing them toward who they are supposed to become.

On weekends, the pace shifted in a way that felt sacred.

There was no rushing out the door for daycare. No alarms pulling us forward. No clock dictating what came next. Those mornings belonged to her. She wandered outside with messy hair and favorite pajamas, barefoot and curious, moving through the yard as if it were an extension of herself.

She plucked tomatoes straight from the vine, juice running down her fingers, sharing pieces with her puppy like it was the most natural thing in the world. There was no urgency. No agenda. Just presence. Just curiosity. Just being.

She moved at her own rhythm.

Unhurried.

Grounded.

Fully alive in the moment.

Those weekends became a classroom of their own.

She learned through dirt and discovery.

I learned through stillness and surrender.

Somewhere in those slow mornings, I realized that this was the energy I wanted to protect. A life with room to breathe. A childhood not constantly rushed or overstimulated. A home where curiosity was allowed to unfold at its own pace. Where wonder was not treated as inefficiency. Where presence was not something you had to earn.

One day, she may not remember the details.

She may not remember the songs I sang off-key, or the way sunlight filtered through the yard on quiet mornings. She may not remember the specific routines or pauses that felt so important to me at the time.

But she will remember how it felt.

The safety.

The warmth.

The sense that she was seen and unhurried and loved.

And I will remember.

I will remember how these tiny moments, so easy to overlook, became the foundation of everything. How they taught me that motherhood is not about capturing the perfect memory, but about being present enough to live it. About noticing what is happening instead of waiting for what comes next.

Tiny moments.

Big love.

And a heart forever changed by the ordinary magic of it all.

For the Mama in It Right Now

If your days feel rushed and your nights feel long, let this land gently.

If you move from one obligation to the next with a running list in your head, wondering whether you are doing enough, whether you are missing something important while trying to keep everything moving, you are not alone. Motherhood often feels like living in motion, like the minutes are always slipping through your hands just as you try to catch them.

If you worry that you are failing because your days are not slow or magical, because they are loud and messy and full of interruption, breathe. Your child feels your presence even in the chaos. They feel it when you pause, even briefly. When you meet their eyes. When you answer a question you have already answered ten times. When you step into their world for a few minutes, even if your mind is still half elsewhere.

They do not need perfection.

They do not need curated moments.

They need you, as you are, showing up imperfectly and repeatedly.

Children do not need parents who never falter. They need parents who return. Who try again. Who stay. You are building a childhood in pieces. In glances. In showing up when it would be easier to disappear into distraction. You are building something real, even when it feels invisible.

You are already giving them what they need.

Even now.

Especially now.

What I Wish I Knew Then

- The small moments were the big ones.
- Slowing down does not have to be constant to be impactful.
- Rushed days do not erase loving ones.
- Children need attention, not perfection.

12

Sick Days That Mothers Don't Get

The first time our daughter got the flu, it arrived without warning.

There was no gradual lead-up, no slow unfolding. One moment she was her usual energetic self, chattering as I laid her down for a nap. The next, something in her body shifted abruptly. She went pale in my arms, her small frame trembling, her eyes wide with confusion as she threw up, really threw up, for the first time in her life.

She did not understand what was happening to her.

She did not know why her stomach hurt, why her body suddenly felt foreign, why the world tilted in a way she could not name. She had never known sickness like this before. She had no context for it, no language for it. All she knew was that something was wrong and that comfort was no longer working the way it always had.

She clung to me, panicked and desperate, searching for relief in the only place she knew how to look.

So I did what mothers do.

I became the safest place she could land.

I held her through every wave of sickness, even when she threw up down my shirt, even when her small body tensed and shook with each surge of nausea. I did not flinch. I did not pull away. I moved instinctively, without thought, as if my body already knew what to do before my mind could catch up. I laid towels across the floor and made a small nest where we could stay close. We slept there together, her body pressed into mine, my arms wrapped around her like a shield I hoped was strong enough.

Every time she whimpered, I rubbed her back and whispered reassurance. Even when I felt powerless. Even when I knew my words could not actually fix what was happening. My heart cracked with every cry she could not explain, every look that begged me to make it stop when I couldn't. There is a particular helplessness that comes with watching your child suffer, knowing that love does not always equal relief.

All I could do was keep her hydrated, hold her close, love her through it, and wait.

It was the longest twenty-four hours of my life.

Time stretches differently when your child is sick. It slows and thickens, bending under the weight of vigilance and fear. Minutes feel endless. Hours blur together. You count breaths without realizing you are doing it. You watch their chest rise and fall. You listen for every sound, terrified of the silence and equally terrified of what might come after it. Sleep comes in fragments, if at all, because your body stays alert even when it is exhausted.

Your nervous system does not rest.

It stands guard.

When morning finally came and she lifted her head with a tired, tentative smile, something inside me loosened. Relief washed through my body. My shoulders dropped. My breath came easier. She was still weak, still recovering, but she was okay. We had made it through the worst of it together.

And then, inevitably, the sickness found me too.

All the close contact, the chest-to-chest soothing, the shared floor sleeping ended the way mothers know it often does. I woke up violently ill the next day, hit with the worst flu I have ever experienced. My body ached in places I forgot could ache. I shivered uncontrollably. My stomach revolted. I lay there bargaining quietly with any higher power that might be listening, asking for strength, for relief, for just a little mercy.

But motherhood does not come with sick days.

Not real ones. Not the kind that existed before children.

Before her, being sick meant rest. It meant calling off work. Curling up in bed. Letting the world move on without me for a day or two. It meant solitude and recovery. Now, rest felt theoretical. Optional at best. Recovery became something I attempted in pieces, between needs and interruptions.

I found myself on the bathroom floor, gripping the toilet with one hand while entertaining my toddler with the other. I would get sick, wipe my face, then sing a song so she would not panic. I set her up with toys on a bathmat, narrating what I was doing between waves of nausea so she would feel safe. I smiled when my body wanted to collapse. I kept my voice steady when my legs shook.

At one point, she toddled over and gently patted my back, mimicking what I had done for her the night before. Trying to help in the only way she knew how.

That moment undid me.

That was motherhood.

Not the polished version.

Not the curated one.

The raw one.

The one where you steady yourself against the counter while they tug at your sleeve. The one where you mother in the narrow spaces between sickness, exhaustion, and survival. The one where love shows up not as patience or grace, but as endurance.

It was the worst flu I have ever had.

And it was also one of the clearest lessons motherhood has given me.

Because even in my misery, my attention never left her. *Was she okay? Did she need anything? Was she drinking enough? Was she warm enough?* The instinct was automatic and nonnegotiable. My body felt broken, but my awareness stayed tethered to her. My suffering did not eclipse my responsibility. It sharpened it.

Being sick as a mother is an entirely different experience. There is no pause button. No stepping fully away. No complete surrender to rest. You show up anyway. You love anyway. You keep going because your child needs you to.

This is true whether you have support or not. Whether someone is home to help or you are doing it alone. Whether you can afford to rest or not. Illness does not pause the needs of a child. And motherhood teaches you, often painfully, that your capacity can stretch far beyond what you once believed possible.

Eventually, we recovered. The towels were washed. The floor was cleaned. The house returned to something resembling normal. The moment passed, as so many do.

But I never forgot that night on the floor or that day on the bathroom tiles.

Those moments taught me that motherhood is not only built

on beauty.

It is built on endurance.

On sacrifice.

On love that shows up when you have nothing left to give.

Because that is what mothers do.

Even when we are sick.

Even when we are exhausted.

Even when we are undone.

We keep showing up.

And somehow, in all its mess and imperfection, that becomes enough.

For the Mama in It Right Now

If you are sitting beside a sick child right now, running on fumes, worrying and aching and wondering how you are supposed to get through another hour, hear this gently. You are not weak for feeling stretched thin. You are human. This is hard in ways no one can fully explain.

Your child does not need you to fix everything. They need you close. Even if all you can offer today is your presence, that is enough. The hours feel endless, the worry feels heavy, but this moment will pass. You are doing something extraordinary in the quietest way.

Rest when you can. Take care of yourself in small ways. Your love is visible even when you feel empty. You are not alone, even if the world has shrunk to a bathroom floor and a tired child in your arms.

What I Wish I Knew Then

- Being sick as a mom is a reminder that you're human, not

a machine.

- The messy, unglamorous moments are the ones that deepen your bond the most.
- You don't have to be strong every second. Your child learns compassion by watching you be real.
- Accepting help is wisdom, not weakness.
- One hard night doesn't define your motherhood, but it does reveal your strength.

13

The Lessons Motherhood Keeps Teaching

Motherhood does not hand you its lessons all at once.

It is not a syllabus. It is not a checklist. There is no moment where you master the material and move on. The lessons arrive in waves. Some settle quietly while you fold laundry that will be unfolded again before the day is over. Some surface as you stand in a doorway watching your child sleep, realizing something has shifted inside you without making a sound. Others crash into you without warning, like a night that stretches longer than you thought you could survive or a moment that cracks you open before you have time to brace yourself.

Some lessons hide inside ordinary days and only reveal themselves later, when you finally have enough distance to understand what you were living through.

For me, motherhood has been a continuous cycle of learning, unlearning, and relearning.

The same truths return again and again, wrapped in different moments, asking me to meet them with more humility each time. Motherhood has softened me, stretched me, humbled me, and rebuilt me in ways I never could have predicted. It has forced me to question everything I once believed about success, about strength, about productivity, about who I thought I needed to be in order to be worthy.

One of the first lessons to surface was the illusion of control.

Before becoming a mother, I believed deeply in planning my way into peace. I color-coded calendars. I mapped routines. I built tidy systems that promised predictability if I followed them closely enough. I treated organization like armor. If I could anticipate enough, I believed I could protect myself from chaos. Preparation felt responsible. Control felt like safety.

Motherhood dismantled that belief quickly.

Not cruelly, but honestly.

No amount of planning could prevent a fever from spiking in the middle of the night. No carefully crafted routine could survive a growth spurt that unraveled every sleep pattern I thought I had finally figured out. No schedule could explain the nights she would only settle if I held her in the dark, rocking back and forth while whispering reassurances I wasn't sure I believed myself.

I remember watching the clock tick forward while nothing changed. My arms ached. My eyes burned. The house was quiet except for her breathing and my own exhaustion. And it hit me then that control was not going to save me. Presence was.

The tighter I tried to grip control, the more everything slipped through my fingers. Eventually, I began to understand that flexibility was not weakness. It was survival. It was wisdom. It was love that could bend without breaking.

Another lesson followed closely behind.

Vulnerability is not a flaw in the foundation.

It *is* the foundation.

There were days I cried openly in front of my partner. Not quietly. Not neatly. The kind of crying that happens when you stop trying to hold yourself together. Days I admitted I didn't have answers. Days I said out loud that I was overwhelmed, that I was scared I was getting it wrong, that I did not know how to carry everything at once.

I expected things to unravel if I let myself be seen like that.

Instead, the opposite happened.

Each time I said, "I need help," I did not lose respect. I gained support. I gained connection. I gained space to breathe. The house did not fall apart. The relationship did not weaken. It deepened.

Vulnerability did not make me weaker.

It made me real.

And being real, I learned, is often where strength actually begins.

As a social worker, the irony was impossible to ignore.

I had spent years supporting parents through crisis. Guiding families through chaos. Teaching about attachment, regulation, and resilience. I knew developmental milestones. I understood trauma responses. I knew what healthy parenting looked like on paper.

And still, motherhood humbled me.

No degree prepares you for the emotional weight of loving a child. There is no training for the way their cry reaches something ancient in you. No professional knowledge shields you from the fear, the tenderness, the responsibility that comes with caring this deeply. Knowing the theory did not spare me from feeling it viscerally. If anything, it made me more aware of how heavy the responsibility feels when love is fully involved.

Asking for help was not failure.

It was survival.

It was humility.

It was love in motion.

I also had to unlearn the myth of the perfect mother.

The calm one.

The organized one.

The one whose home is always presentable, whose meals are balanced, whose child never melts down in public, whose emotions are always regulated.

That mother does not exist.

What exists are real mothers. Mothers who are tired and messy and stretched thin. Mothers who love fiercely and still lose their patience. Mothers who apologize. Mothers who repair. Mothers who show up again after a hard moment and try again.

I stopped chasing the image and started honoring the reality. Motherhood is not about perfection. It is about presence. It is about repair. It is about staying connected when things fall apart.

Somewhere along the way, I relearned the importance of small victories.

Victories that would have gone unnoticed in any other chapter of my life. A nap finally taken after hours of resistance. A belly laugh so intense it turned into hiccups. A new word spoken at exactly the right moment. A spontaneous dance party in the kitchen. A tantrum survived without losing myself. A moment when she reached for me without hesitation, as if my arms were the safest place she had ever known.

These moments taught me that life does not need to be extraordinary to be meaningful.

Motherhood is a masterclass in patience, resilience, perspective, and radical acceptance. And you do not pass the class once and move on. You learn it on repeat.

There are days when I miss the version of myself from before motherhood.

The one with more freedom.

More sleep.

More certainty.

The one who could leave the house without planning around naps. The one who could sit in silence without listening for a cry. Those longings still visit me sometimes, but they are gentler now. Because I have come to understand that the woman I am now, the one who sings off-key lullabies, who navigates chaos, who finds beauty in mess, who softens at the sound of a small voice calling her name, is someone I never could have met without becoming a mother.

Motherhood is messy.

It is relentless.

It is beautiful.

It is transformative.

The lessons do not arrive neatly packaged. They come in laughter and tears. In breakthroughs and breakdowns. In clarity that fades and returns again. Nothing about it is linear. Nothing about it is perfect.

And somehow, that is exactly what makes it sacred.

One evening, after a day that did not go the way I planned, I found myself sitting on the floor of her room while she played nearby. Toys were scattered everywhere. Dinner had been rushed. The house felt louder than I wanted it to be. I felt the familiar urge to stand up, to fix something, to restore order before moving on.

Instead, I stayed.

She brought me a book I had already read too many times, climbed into my lap, and waited. I read slowly. She interrupted constantly. We laughed when I messed up the words. At one point, she rested her head against my chest, not because she was tired, but because she wanted to be close.

The mess remained.

The to-do list waited.

But in that moment, nothing was missing.

Later, when I finally stood up, I realized something quietly profound. I had not fixed the day. I had lived it. And somehow, that was enough.

I am not the woman I was before.

I am not the woman I thought I would be.

I am someone entirely new.

I have been cracked open, reshaped, rebuilt, and deeply softened by love. And I would not trade a single lesson. Not one.

As I softened and rebuilt myself, something else emerged quietly but powerfully. The more I learned about who I was becoming, the more I learned about who I refused to be ever again.

Motherhood did not just teach me vulnerability.

It taught me bravery.

It taught me boundaries.

It taught me that I am allowed to take up space.

I was no longer willing to shrink myself for other people's comfort.

Something in me had risen.

And that shift changed everything.

For the Mama in It Right Now

If you are standing in the middle of your own learning curve, overwhelmed, stretched thin, and quietly wondering if you are doing any of it right, I hope you pause long enough to offer yourself grace. You were never meant to know everything from the start. You were never meant to carry every answer in your pocket. You are allowed to grow into this slowly, messily, beautifully.

You are allowed to ask for help without turning it into a confession of failure. You are allowed to cry without making it mean you are not strong. You are allowed to rest without earning it. You are allowed to change your mind, to soften your expectations, to loosen your grip on control one white knuckled finger at a time.

Some days will feel like progress. Some days will feel like survival. Both count. Both matter. You are doing sacred work, even on the days that feel like failure. Especially on those days. Motherhood is not an exam. It is an evolution. And you are learning in real time, which means you are doing it exactly the way it was always meant to be done.

What I Wish I Knew Then:

- Perfection and control were never the goal. Connection was.
- Asking for help is not weakness. It is wisdom.
- No mother gets through this without breaking down sometimes.
- Small victories are the heartbeats of motherhood.
- I would not lose myself. I would meet a new version of myself.

- Motherhood would teach me more than any degree ever could.

14

Boundaries, Cycle-Breaking, and Becoming

Becoming a mother did not just stretch me emotionally.

It rewired my backbone.

The world did not suddenly become louder, but I heard it differently. The stakes shifted. The lens through which I saw people, decisions, and expectations sharpened almost overnight. Things I once tolerated without question began to feel heavy in my hands. What used to feel manageable now felt misaligned. What I once explained away no longer made sense.

Motherhood has a way of doing that. It strips life down to what actually matters. It removes the excess and exposes the truth underneath. And in that stripping away, something quietly ended for me. Something I had carried for years without realizing how deeply it shaped my choices.

Motherhood ended my people pleasing.

Before my daughter, I bent myself into shapes that made other people comfortable. I swallowed discomfort to keep the peace. I stayed quiet to avoid conflict. I learned how to read a room and adjust myself accordingly, smoothing tension before anyone else had to feel it. I treated other people's discomfort as my responsibility to manage. That instinct had once helped me navigate families, expectations, and systems where harmony was valued more than honesty.

But motherhood changed the cost of that instinct entirely.

Because suddenly, there were little eyes watching. Little ears listening. A child learning not just from my words, but from my silence. And the thought of her growing up believing she had to make herself smaller to be loved shifted something in me completely.

Motherhood held a mirror up to my life and asked a question I could not ignore.

Is this who you want your child to learn from.

How could I teach her that her body mattered if I did not protect it.

How could I teach her that boundaries were real if I allowed mine to be crossed.

How could I teach her that her safety came first if I prioritized other people's comfort.

The shift did not arrive all at once. It came in moments. Practical ones. Ordinary ones. The kind that look small from the outside but feel seismic when you are the one holding the line.

It looked like asking people to wash their hands before holding her, even when they brushed it off as unnecessary. It looked like saying no to kisses on her face, no matter how affectionate or well intentioned the request seemed. It looked like standing firm when someone laughed and said, "We did this with our kids and they turned out fine."

I stopped explaining.

I stopped defending.

I simply repeated myself.

This is what we are doing.

It showed up in feeding decisions too. In choosing how and when to introduce foods. In saying no to peanuts and popcorn before she was developmentally ready, even when others insisted we were being overly cautious. It showed up in limiting unsolicited advice disguised as concern, in learning to say, "We've got it handled," without softening the edges or adding apologies.

And it showed up in decisions that carried far more weight than I expected.

Vaccination was one of them.

My boyfriend and I were both vaccinated. It was not something we debated endlessly or agonized over. It was a decision shaped by trust in science, lived experience, and the understanding that protecting ourselves had always been about more than just us. When our daughter was born, choosing to vaccinate her felt like a continuation of that same responsibility. Thoughtful. Intentional. Grounded.

And still, it was not simple.

Parenthood has a way of turning even well considered decisions into points of tension. Suddenly, your choices are no longer just yours. They are examined. Questioned. Interpreted. Held up against other people's fears, beliefs, and experiences. What felt clear inside our home became complicated the moment it stepped outside of it.

Some extended family members disagreed with our choice.

At first, the differences felt manageable. A comment here. A question there. Curiosity framed as concern. But over time, it escalated. Studies were shared. Articles posted. Social media became a quiet battleground where opinions were broadcast publicly instead of discussed privately. Research appeared in conversations that were never invitations for debate.

It was exhausting.

Not because we doubted our decision, but because we were constantly being asked to defend it. Parenthood already asks you to justify yourself in a thousand invisible ways. Adding this layer felt like being pulled into a conversation that never ended.

I learned quickly that vaccine conversations are rarely just about vaccines.

They are about trust. About fear. About autonomy. About who feels heard and who feels dismissed. About generational differences and the illusion of control in a world that already feels uncertain.

For us, the choice to vaccinate was about protection. Not just of our child, but of the wider community she would move through. Schools. Daycare centers. Grocery stores. Doctor's offices. The invisible web of people we are all connected to, including those who cannot be vaccinated themselves.

From a community perspective, vaccination is collective.

From a family perspective, it is deeply personal.

Disagreements like this do not live neatly on paper. They live at dinner tables. In group texts. In pauses that stretch too long after a comment lands too hard. They surface between parents and grandparents, siblings and cousins, friends who once felt aligned and suddenly feel distant.

And with action came boundaries.

That was a lesson motherhood taught me quickly. You can respect someone's autonomy without surrendering your responsibility.

We learned to disengage when conversations became heated.

To share information only when it felt invited. To remember that preserving relationships sometimes meant stepping back rather than trying to win understanding.

But we did not shrink our decision to make others more comfortable.

Because motherhood clarified something fundamental for me. Protecting my child is not a debate. It is a commitment. One that asks for courage, steadiness, and the willingness to disappoint people you care about.

That lesson extended beyond health.

It showed up in privacy. We asked that no photos of our baby be shared on social media before we had the chance to announce her birth ourselves. Her arrival deserved intention, not immediacy. Holding that boundary disappointed people who were excited to share joy publicly. We held it anyway.

It showed up in time. We decided early on that no matter what, our family would spend Christmas Eve and Christmas morning together at home. No rushing. No splitting time. No performing. Just us.

Because we understood something then that we could not unsee. What you tolerate around your child becomes the emotional air they breathe. What you prioritize teaches them what matters.

My boyfriend and I built this clarity together. Through conversations that were not always easy. Through moments that required honesty instead of avoidance. Somewhere along the way, we made a decision that became foundational.

We will not let anyone, not friends or the family we came from, destroy the family we are creating.

That decision is not rooted in bitterness. It is rooted in awareness. Unhealthy patterns do not disappear simply because we hope they will. They enter quietly through small allowances if we let them.

There were moments when people pushed back. When boundaries were questioned. When our choices were labeled excessive or sensitive. When we had to choose between keeping peace with others or keeping peace in our home.

Every time, we chose our daughter.

People say we have changed. That we are distant. That we are rigid. They do not see the way we look at each other when hard decisions have to be made. They do not see how unified we are. How deeply we protect what we are building. How we back each other without hesitation.

That is partnership. Not the kind that only works on easy days, but the kind that stands firm when things get uncomfortable.

It still amazes me how often families confuse silence with peace. Tiptoeing around volatility is not harmony. It is fear disguised as calm. Real peace is when everyone feels respected. Real peace is emotional safety. Real peace is honesty paired with boundaries.

I refuse to raise my daughter in an environment where conflict avoidance matters more than her sense of security. I want her to know that protecting her energy is not something she ever has to apologize for. I want her to understand that the people who call you difficult are often the ones who benefited most from your silence.

And when it comes to safety, I am unwavering.

If anyone ever says to my child, "Don't tell your mom," we will have an immediate problem. Safe adults do not ask children to keep secrets from their parents. In our home, surprises are fine. Surprises include everyone. Secrets do not.

Motherhood taught me that it is not my job to be liked.

For most of my life, likability felt like safety. Approval felt like protection. Motherhood dismantled that belief completely. It taught me that my role is not to make everyone else comfortable. It is to be anchored. To be steady enough that my child has something solid to grow against.

When it comes to our child, her well being will always come before someone else's comfort. That truth does not bend.

Call it intense.

Call it protective.

Call it whatever you want.

I call it intentional parenting.

I am gentle. I lead with empathy. But I am not passive when harm walks in. I will speak. I will intervene. I will protect.

If someone disrespects my child, ignores her boundaries, or makes her feel small, their title does not excuse it. Family does not excuse it. Love does not require endurance of harm.

We are not raising a child who learns to survive dysfunction.

We are raising a child who expects better.

And because she is watching me, I expect better too.

I am not raising a child to fit comfortably into the world.

I am raising a child who knows her worth.

And in the process, I finally learned mine.

For the Mama in It Right Now

If you are in the season where you are learning to speak up, to set boundaries that feel unfamiliar on your tongue, to say no even when your voice trembles, give yourself credit. This is not small work. It is brave, disruptive, necessary work. It feels uncomfortable not because it is wrong, but because it is new. You are unlearning patterns that once kept you safe and replacing them with choices that protect your child now.

You are allowed to reclaim your voice. You are allowed to prioritize safety over silence, clarity over politeness, and peace over people pleasing. You are allowed to choose your child and yourself even when others interpret that choice as distance, defiance, or change. Growth often looks like disruption from the outside. That does not make it unkind. It makes it honest.

If guilt rises, pause with it. Guilt is often the echo of old conditioning. It shows up when you stop being easy to manage. When you stop shrinking to keep others comfortable. When you no longer abandon yourself to maintain approval. Guilt does not mean you are doing harm. Often, it means you are doing something different. Something healthier. Something that would have once felt impossible.

You are allowed to be the first generation to say, "This ends with me."

The first to choose boundaries over obligation.

The first to teach that love does not require endurance of harm.

The first to model what self respect looks like in real time.

Your child is watching you. Not just in the big moments, but in the quiet ones. In the way you speak up. In the way you pause instead of shrinking. In the way you protect your peace without apology. They are learning what it looks like to trust themselves by watching you learn to trust yourself.

That is not selfish.

That is not cold.

That is not failure.

That is legacy work.

That is courage in motion.

That is love made visible.

And you are doing it, one choice at a time.

What I Wish I Knew Then

- Saying no is not disrespectful. Sometimes it is necessary.
- Boundaries do not push healthy people away. They reveal who benefited from your lack of them.
- Choosing my child's safety over someone's comfort is never wrong.
- Modeling strength teaches your child strength.
- Motherhood would give me courage I could not build on my own.

15

The Hope That Grew Roots

Before my daughter was born, hope was something I handled carefully. It felt fragile, conditional, easily startled. I learned to keep it quiet, to tuck it away where it could not disappoint me too deeply if things did not unfold the way I imagined. Hope lived in small, almost private moments then. In thoughts I did not say out loud. In pauses I did not linger in. It looked like scrolling baby name lists and pretending it was casual. Like standing in a store aisle a few seconds too long, staring at tiny socks, then walking away before the wanting could root itself too deeply. I believed just enough to get through the day, but not enough to feel exposed.

I hoped to become a mother.

Not in a vague, someday sense, but in a way that settled into my body and became part of my internal language. I hoped for a life that felt fuller and more anchored. I hoped to love someone in a way that felt bigger than me. I hoped for ordinary things. Bedtime routines. Little shoes by the door. A child who would call me mama. I hoped for a future where the hard parts would make sense because there was love waiting at the center of it all.

When she arrived, tiny and fierce and entirely herself, hope did not disappear. It changed. It deepened. It grew roots.

Once she was here, hope stopped being something I held delicately and became something I carried with responsibility. Not the heavy kind that weighs you down, but the sacred kind that steadies you. Hope became less about what I wanted and more about what I was willing to build. It became active. Intentional. Something that stretched beyond me and planted itself firmly in her future.

In her first year of life, my hope for her was simple. I hoped she felt safe. Safe in arms that never tired of holding her. Safe in voices that always came back. Safe in a world that responded to her needs with care instead of impatience. I hoped she learned, without being taught, that her presence mattered. That when she cried, someone came. That when she reached, she was met. That love was reliable.

I hoped her days were filled with wonder. Tiny discoveries that felt monumental. Belly laughs that arrived without warning. Messy moments that left evidence of joy everywhere they landed. I hoped she learned that it was okay to cry, to need help, to take her time becoming who she was meant to be. That growth did not require urgency. That she was allowed to move through the world at her own pace.

As she grew, my hopes grew with her.

I hoped she would know her own strength and learn to love without borders. I hoped she would dream boldly and read books that expanded her sense of what was possible. When people told her she was pretty, I hoped she would know it was more than her looks. I hoped she would know she was smart. That she was kind. That her voice mattered and her mind deserved to be seen.

As she grows into herself, I hope she stands strong. I know there will be moments when the world tries to knock her down. I hope she holds on then. I hope she understands that her power cannot be measured. That her passion and vulnerability are not weaknesses, but things to be protected and treasured. I hope she learns the difference between right and wrong not because of rules imposed on her, but because she listens to what lives in her own heart. I hope she questions narratives that do not fit. That she speaks clearly. That she never repeats herself out of doubt or fear.

I hope she strives for big things in a world that often asks women to shrink. I hope she knows that worth is not measured by size, silence, or compliance. I hope she stands up for those who need it, herself included. I hope she believes she is allowed to take up space.

She has been loved like this since the beginning. Before she had a name. Before she took her first breath. Before she understood words or expectations or the shape of the world. This love is not conditional. It is not fragile. It is not something she can lose. She will never have to earn it or perform for it. It is constant.

I hope she grows up seeing a mother who is imperfect and honest about it. A mother who keeps showing up, even when she feels unsure. A mother whose strength does not need to announce itself. The kind that apologizes when she is wrong. The kind that tries again without needing credit. I hope she sees me choose presence over perfection, peace over proving a point, integrity over comparison. Not because I want her to witness struggle, but because I want her to understand that a meaningful life does not require flawlessness. It requires honesty, resilience, and a willingness to keep your heart open.

There is a tenderness in holding hope for someone who does not yet understand how big the world is. Some nights, I look at her and feel the ache of it. Not fear rooted in doubt, but the kind that comes from loving someone more than your own comfort. I know I cannot protect her from everything. I know pain and disappointment will find her eventually. But I can give her a home that feels steady. I can be anchored enough to be her soft place when the world gets sharp.

She does not know it yet, but she is held by a love she will never have to question. A lifetime of me showing up. A lifetime of warm hugs in the kitchen and long talks in the car that begin as errands and turn into everything. A lifetime of reminders that she is never alone. A lifetime of pride that celebrates her wins as if they are my own. A lifetime of care that aches when her heart hurts. A lifetime of love that does not shrink as she grows.

The hope that once carried me toward her now carries me forward with her. Into every tomorrow we will share. Hand in hand. Heart to heart. Growing and becoming together.

As I look toward her future, I cannot help but reflect on my own path. How different it was from the one I once imagined. How many turns it took. How much becoming it required. And that is when the truth settled in.

There is not just one way to become a mother.

There are a million.

And every single one is worthy of hope.

For the Mama in It Right Now

If you are in the season of dreaming for your child while still learning how to stand in this new version of yourself, let this meet you gently. The hopes you carry are not fragile or foolish. They are not something you have to justify or earn by doing everything right first. They exist because you love deeply. Because you can already see your child as more than this moment, more than this stage. Because you believe their future matters.

If today feels messy, if the house is loud, if patience ran thin and you had to circle back with an apology, know this. Your child is not being shaped by a single hard moment. They are being shaped by your return. By the way you keep showing up. By the way you repair, reconnect, and choose them again, even when you are tired or unsure.

You do not need to have it all figured out for your child to feel safe. You do not need to be calm every day or confident in every decision for them to feel loved. Your presence teaches them security. Your tenderness teaches them softness. Your boundaries teach them safety. Your effort, imperfect and human, teaches them what devotion looks like.

If you are still finding your footing while holding hope for the kind of person your child might become, you are not behind. You are not failing. You are becoming. And that becoming is happening right alongside your child's.

Hope does not have to be loud to be powerful. It can live quietly in the way you hold them. In the way you speak their name. In the way you imagine goodness for them even when the days feel heavy.

Your child feels that hope.

And it is enough.

What I Wish I Knew Then

- The hope I carried before motherhood would evolve into something deeper and steadier.
- I did not need to be perfect for my child to feel safe and completely loved.
- Kindness, softness, and strength could coexist in one day, sometimes in one moment.
- Modeling self love would matter more than any speech I could give.
- The love I felt before she existed was only the beginning.

16

A Million Paths to Motherhood

The longer I live inside motherhood, the more stories I hear.

Not the polished ones. Not the tidy versions shared at baby showers or folded neatly into social media captions. I hear the real ones. The stories that come out in fragments. In quiet confessions whispered over cold coffee. In late night messages that begin with, "Can I be honest for a minute?" In the pauses before someone admits that this is harder, lonelier, or more complicated than they expected.

And the more stories I hear, the more certain I become of this truth.

There is not one way to become a mother.

There are a million.

Some women follow a path that looks exactly like the one they imagined. Dating. Marriage. Pregnancy. Baby. A sequence that unfolds in a familiar order, supported by tradition and reinforced by expectation. Others walk a far more winding road. One shaped by infertility and appointments that blur together. By months measured in cycles and hope that has learned to be careful. Some become mothers through adoption, choosing love with intention and courage, opening their homes and hearts to children who arrive through loss and resilience. Some plan meticulously. Some wait patiently. Some are surprised. Some become mothers after miscarriage or stillbirth, carrying grief alongside joy in ways that permanently change the shape of both. Some step into motherhood in ways the world does not always recognize or honor, and they do it anyway.

Every story is different.

Every story is real.

Every story counts.

My path was not tidy. It did not follow the order I once believed it should. It was shaped by PCOS and uncertainty. By love that unfolded before marriage. By conversations that were honest and hard. By fear and humor, resilience and tears. It was marked by moments of deep doubt and moments of quiet knowing. I cried more than I expected. I laughed harder than I thought possible. I learned how to live in the in between spaces. Between expectation and reality. Between control and surrender. Between the life I planned and the one that arrived anyway.

I had to make peace with the fact that my story did not match the version I once assumed I would tell.

I had to let go of the belief that motherhood needed to look a certain way to be legitimate. I had to release the idea that there was a correct order that granted approval, safety, or worth. I learned that love does not require a perfect introduction. Love shows up in the middle of imperfection and builds something meaningful there. Love does not ask for a clean narrative. Love asks for presence.

That, I have learned, is the point.

Motherhood is not defined by the path you took to get here. It is defined by the way you show up once you arrive. Planned or unplanned. Smooth or chaotic. Celebrated or complicated. The meaning is not in getting it right. It is in choosing your child again and again. On the days when your body is tired. On the days when your patience runs thin. On the days when your heart feels stretched beyond what you thought it could hold.

And it is also in choosing yourself.

Because a mother is still a person, even when the world sometimes forgets that. Becoming mama is my story. It is not perfect or linear or quiet, but it is real. It is shaped by love and struggle, humor and fear, exhaustion and awe. It is a story of learning and unlearning, of holding contradictions at once, of becoming someone new while still honoring the woman I was before. It is made up of moments that broke me open and moments that stitched me back together, often in the same breath.

This book was never meant to tell you how your motherhood should look. It was never meant to offer timelines, rules, or answers that fit neatly into a checklist. It was meant to name how motherhood can feel. The heartbreak and the humor. The grief and the joy. The invisible labor. The small victories no one claps for. The days you feel like you are coming undone and the moments you realize you are stronger than you ever imagined.

Your path matters.

The way you mother matters.

The way you love, protect, worry, show up, repair, and try again matters far more than milestones or comparisons. Far more than curated celebrations or perfect photos. Far more than the version of motherhood someone else decided should be the standard.

Motherhood is not a destination you arrive at fully formed or fully prepared. It is a relationship. A process. A continual becoming that unfolds one ordinary, extraordinary day at a time. There is not a single right way to walk it. There is only your way. Your messy, beautiful, imperfect, deeply human way.

And it is enough.

Wherever you are on your journey, whether you are waiting or struggling, celebrating or grieving, beginning again or starting over, know this. Your story is valid. Your love is real. Your effort matters. And somehow, in all the chaos and quiet, in all the laughter and tears, you are exactly where you are meant to be.

You are a mother.

A protector.

A teacher.

A nurturer.

A human being doing her best.

So hold your child close. And hold yourself close too. Celebrate the small victories. Forgive the missteps. Release the need for perfection. There is no finish line here. No blueprint. No prize for doing it all right. There is only showing up, again and again, with love that stretches wider than fear, with courage that rises even when you feel unsure, with a heart that keeps learning, giving, and becoming.

Motherhood is not a performance, a test, or a checklist. It is a lifetime of moments that matter, even when no one is watching. And in those moments, in your presence, your persistence, and your imperfect, extraordinary love, you are doing exactly what you were always meant to do.

You are walking your own path. It may not look like anyone

else's, and it does not need to. It is shaped by love, by effort, by the countless times you chose to keep going.

And this is not the end of the story.

Motherhood does not stop once you arrive.

It keeps unfolding.

It keeps stretching you.

It keeps asking you to grow.

This book closes here.

But the becoming continues.

Still becoming.

Every day.

For the Mama in It Right Now:

Wherever you are on your journey, whether you are holding a newborn, chasing a toddler, waiting for a positive test, healing from loss, navigating uncertainty, or loving a child who arrived in a way you never planned for, I want you to hear this clearly. Your path is yours for a reason. There is no timeline you are behind on and no version of motherhood you have failed to live up to. You are not late. You are not less. And you are not doing it wrong simply because your story does not resemble someone else's.

If your days feel messy or overwhelming, if your emotions feel close to the surface, or if this season looks nothing like what you imagined it would, that does not mean you are failing. It means you are living inside something real. It means you are learning how to hold love, responsibility, and identity all at once. It means you are becoming someone new while still carrying the woman you have always been.

If you feel worn down by comparison, by subtle judgment, or by the quiet pressure to explain or justify your choices, I hope you allow yourself to set that weight down. You do not owe anyone a polished version of your motherhood. You do not need to defend how you got here or prove that you belong. Your place is not earned through performance. It already exists because of your love.

Your child will not remember how closely you followed someone else's example. They will remember how it felt to be with you. The way you returned when things were hard. The way you kept showing up, even when you were unsure. Your presence, not your perfection, is what stays.

And if you are in a season where hope feels delicate, where grief still sits nearby, or where the path ahead feels uncertain, let this be your reminder. You are allowed to move slowly. You are allowed to need support. You are allowed to rest. You are allowed to hope, even if you can only hold it carefully right now.

You are enough, even on the days that feel heavy and unsteady. Especially on the days that feel like too much.

What I Wish I Knew Then:

- No two motherhood stories look the same, and comparison only steals joy.
- The path to becoming a mother is not supposed to be perfect. It is supposed to be lived.
- Detours, delays, heartbreaks, and unexpected turns can still lead you exactly where you are meant to be.
- Nothing about your story makes you behind. There is no single blueprint.
- The version of motherhood you imagined before it happened will change, and you will change too.

137

- Your worth as a mother has nothing to do with how you got here and everything to do with the love you give now.
- You were enough long before you ever believed it.